ANCHOR BOOKS

WORDS FROM WITHIN

First published in Great Britain in 1994 by
ANCHOR BOOKS
1-2 Wainman Road, Woodston,
Peterborough, PE2 7BU

All Rights Reserved

Copyright Contributors 1994

Foreword

Anchor Books is a small press, established in 1992, with the aim of promoting readable poetry to as wide an audience as possible.

We hope to establish an outlet for writers of poetry who may have struggled to see their work in print.

Following our request in the National Press, we were overwhelmed by the response. The poems presented here have been selected from many entries. Editing proved to be a difficult and daunting task and as the Editor, the final selection was mine.

The poems chosen represent a cross-section of styles and content. They have been sent from all over the country, written by young and old alike, united in the passion for writing poetry.

I trust this selection will delight and please the authors and all those who enjoy reading poetry.

Glenn Jones
Editor

CONTENTS

Memories	D Owen	1
Ladies Who Lunch	Deirdre J Cameron	2
Cottage On The Pier	Catherine Neale	3
Love's Ambiguity	D M Fink	4
The Children Who Stay	Richard Leduchowicz	5
Life?	Ivy Allpress	6
Dreams And Thoughts	Julie Mears	7
Childhood	Gwynneth Curtis	8
A Sense Of Taste	Lawrence Stewart	9
The Tramp	Esme Francis	10
Regret	Nahieda Bi	11
To A Special Lady	Mary Adamson	12
What We Deserve?	Paula Holdstock	13
The Ramblers	Paul Swaffer	14
Our Customer Jack	Donna Louisa Caldwell	15
If Only The Ashes Could Speak . . .	Barbara J Niemienionek-Lindsay	16
Empathy	Paul Hutton	18
That's Life	Wilf Lawrence	19
Mother Nature's Complain	Martin Forman	20
Waves	Rose Hosking	21
Priceless	Andy Botterill	22
Great Expectations!	John Goldsbrough	23
Sand Of Time	B Jones	24
Teardrops	Carol Anne Burnup	25
The Railway Child	Mary Hayworth	26
Silver Rain	George Pearson	27
The Sounder	John Noble	28
The Flower Show	V N King	29
In My Attic	Sue Jackson	30
Directional Thoughts	A Bacon	31
The Factory Worker	David Kennedy	32
A Moment In Eternity	David Bridgewater	33
Changing Face Of Nature	Sarah Maycock	34
The Scottish Cup Final - 1994	David Wilson	35

Our Little Piece Of Heaven	Rosemary Thomson	36
The World Through A Little Boy's Eyes	Chris Hamlin	37
Reflections	David Cooper	38
Hardship Builds Character - But Loneliness Builds Walls	Rosalyn Carr	39
The Hedge	Peggy Love	40
The Foaming Sea	Alan Mitchell	41
Caledonian Isles	Richard Stewart	42
Thursday Nights	Cath Cunningham	43
Willow	John Arnold	44
A Student's Lament	Barbara Wheatley	45
With Love Each Day	Shirley Boyson	46
The Clown	Raymond Fenech	48
Sunset	L Smith-Warren	49
A Brave Face	Michael Webb	50
Look Up	A B Hughes	51
The Greatest Game?	Carol Spellman	52
Gliding To What Should Have Been	Gill Oliver	53
The Girls' Night Out	Sharon Utting	54
In My Spare Time . . .	Paula E O'Connor	55
Out Again	Dominique Woolf	56
My Theatre Treat	P E Taylor	57
A Complete Knit!	Claire Morgan	58
City Moon	Ian Duckett	59
The Beauty Battle	Sarah Robinson	60
Time To Spare	Mary Stirling	61
Time Of My Own	Margaret Laws	62
Friends	Nuala Fitzpatrick	63
Quality Leisure	V Buchan	64
Things We Get Up To	J Melling	65
The Bootfair Punter	Joan Sharrocks	66
Just Another Day	Joyce M Hefti-Whitney	67
Neighbours	Corinne Patty	69
Anon	Trudie Gordon	70
Inside Out	Claire Hart	71
The Hand That Controls You	Rachel Oliver	72

Spare Time	D E Roderick	73
Victim Of Addiction	Russell Dandy	74
Joshua	Fiona Gibb	75
Man-Kind	Joyeeta Mukherjee	76
Abandon Ship	Elizabeth Melvin	77
A Prayer To God	Fiona Donocik	78
Sunday At The Piper	Tracey Sharp	79
Grandpa	Amanda L Wilson	80
Colours Of Love	Caroline Phillips	81
Touched By Love	Rosemarie F Lockyer	82
The Tragedy Queen	Stephanie Francis	83
A Girls's Night Out	Zoe Woods	84
Aerobics	Jane Elizabeth Drew	85
Happy Times	A M Bolton	86
Untitled	Jackie Lines	87
Patch	Laura McCloskey	88
Don't Lose Control	Rebecca Pritchard	89
Houseboat	Trudie Gordon	90
Forty Winks	Diane Lavery	91
Turn Loose The Days	David Collyer	92
Lonely	Kate Bradley	93
Boko	Rebbecca Rampton	94
Untitled	Lorna Hirst	95
Staying Abreast	Zoe Simmons	96
Bye-Bye Baby	Sonia Phillips	97
A Mother's Child	Mavis Henderson	98
Untitled	Simone Bertrand	99
To Daddy	A Hyndman	100
Fit For What	Ian C Dayer	101
Thank You To Reg	Neta Holmes	102
Untitled	C Rawlinson	103
Rhapsody To The Memory Of B Baker	Simon Hall	104
Eastenders	S McGill	105
Bobby's Gone Away	Janette Turner	106
Dear Percy	Nicola Scott	107
A Soap Fan	Chris Maddison	108
Eastenders - Albert Square	Mollie D Earl	109

Brookside	Kirsteen Sinclair	110
Den And Angie Watts - Eastenders	Stephanie Davies	111
Brookside	Bobby MacDuff	112
Soad Addict?	Rachel Robinson	113
The Pub To The Shed	Jean Spearing	114
Untitled	Debbie Dulieu	115
War Of The Soaps	R Butler	116
Neighbours	Irene Clegg	117
Brookside	Dorothy M Arrowsmith	118
The Street	E Wilson	119
Poem On Soaps	Kay M Reid	121
Coronation Street	D Ayshford	122
The TV Soaps	Nancy Smith	123
Carly Parker's View Towards TV Soaps	Carly Parker	124
The Street	Jean Buckmaster	125
Soaps	A G Holmes	126
Soap Folk	Augusta Waite	127
These Three Soaps Are For Me	A Ashley	128
Untitled	G Pughsley	129
All My Soaps	Pam Harrison	130
My Normal Day	Lynn McAuley	131
The Marksman	Ann Rutherford	132
The Busker	Tracey Ross	133
Fate	David Quick	134
Lonely Friends	Roger Stokes	135
Mother	C Bampton	136
Spare Time	Susan O'Shea	137
Who Knows	Roseann Standring	138
It All Starts Here	Lisa Wakeham	140
Deep In My Soul	Rachel Imm	141
When Lovers Sleep	Mandy Chambers	142
Country Lovers	Jennifer Jenkins	143
The Geranium	B Pritchard	144
Chosen	Driekje de Boer	145
Forever In Your Heart	David McMahon	146

Country Cameos	Margaret Barns	147
Priceless	J Maitland	148
The Summer Has Come	Stefanie Thomas	149
Untitled	Sally Humphries	150
The World Spins Round	Stephen O'Toole	151
Spiritual Faith	Janette Homer	152
Beyond The Veil	Dorothy Walker	153
Restorative Power	Lisbeth Cameron	154
Country Walks	Doreen Higgs	155
Rescue Dog	A Janes	156
A Shadow Never Seen	Jack Ellis	157
A March Day In Methwold	P Holt	158
Butterfly	Alison White	159
I Had To Set Him Free	Catherine Barrons	160
The Nature Game	Audrey Forbes-Handley	161
Brass Band In Muker	Ron Woollard	162

MEMORIES

When I think back and remember
All the times we had.
I can only remember the good ones
'Cause we never had any bad.

You always had a joke to tell
A smile you'd always wear.
A caring heart you had inside
So much love you had to share.

I thought we'd be a couple
Who'd live life to the top.
But something got in our way
Now the pain will never stop.

You had to go and be with her
The one who has your son.
But your love is with me always
'Cause for me you're the only one.

D Owen

LADIES WHO LUNCH

Ladies who lunch like to wear Jacques Vert.
Do you think that this jacket matches that skirt?
You can call for coffee let's say about ten
I'll probably be ready just around then.

We'll visit the boutique that Liz has acquired
Oh shopping can make me feel rather tired.
There's a dear little wine bar that's painted dark green
The Chardonnay good and the chicken supreme.

We can sit for an hour and do nothing but chat.
Oh my God fancy her wearing something like that!
I didn't think Claire would leave Dennis for Jim
Of course it's the fashion to be living in sin.

My goodness I'm sorry I cannot be late
Tim and Camille will be at the school gate.
They go to the prep school you know called St Bees
It's a struggle my dear to keep paying the fees.

Camille is dancing the lead in Swan Lake.
I love ballet you know, I go there for her sake.
There's tennis in summer and pony club too
I think children nowadays need plenty to do.

I've got an appointment with Monsieur Jean-Pierre
He's excellent my darling at colouring hair.
I'll get the beautician to pain my nails pink
They'll match my new evening dress better I think.

I'll see you tonight at the charity bash
It should be good fun and raise lots of cash.
This country needs people like you and like me
They spend their time wisely and do good works for free.

Deirdre J Cameron

COTTAGE ON THE PIER

Ancient timbered rooms, what secrets you
could tell, sounds of sea, summer nights,
an winter mists, soft with candlelight,
Tall ships seen from your windows, majestic
sails unfurled, saw you then as still you
stand, welcoming the sailor home again.
Time and tide have dealt well with you,
bygone days long out of sight, echoing the
remembered hours, laughter, births, and deaths,
and bridal nights.
Changing time like the passing ships have
seen you stay serene, all your ghosts are
happy ones of those who have gone before,
Aged timeless little house, built on the
Harbour's shore.

Catherine Neale

LOVE'S AMBIGUITY

Where does love go?
Does it die with the loved one?
Or does it continue in what lies beyond?

Does the ache ever cease?
Is that what is wanted
By the one who is left with the shatters of dreams?

Dreams may not come true
For some it must be so,
But is there regret for what never can be?

If dreams never were -
If love never came -
We'd live with the absence of both joy and pain.

The ache is exquisite -
The pain bittersweet -
The memory poignant, forever in capture -
Soul mates of delight, elation and rapture.

D M Fink

THE CHILDREN WHO STAY

I've lived by the Primary School
For many years
Listened to the same child
Heard the laughter and tears
Seen the innocence of play
And heard the dreaded stop
Of discipline,
When friendship is made
In polite address
But teasing mischief
With races along the public path.

When children describe
How their day was won or lost
To inquisitive parents
Amid stories
Of eagerly awaited dinners.

When time is many years
A child never really leaves school
At all.

Richard Leduchowicz

LIFE?

The philosopher sits in his high-back chair
and wonders why.
You and I we struggle on
and often cry.
And endless battle it always seem,
the philosopher sits and reads his reams,
while you and I we dream our dreams,
and still struggle on.

We strive and strain.
Why do we do it?
What ever it is
we are bound to rue it.
What drives us on against all odds
that fate has got in store.
Is it the laughter of the gods
that makes us struggle more.
Or is it a flame which burns within in
a steady constant source
inspiring us to carry on
in our appointed course.

Ivy Allpress

DREAMS AND THOUGHTS

Precious as when your eyes
are the colours of your dreams
and your dreams
are like trees
strong and tall
with dappled leaves
sharing life and growth
as the swallow beats its heart
on its soaring wings
to capture the
fluid breathing beauty
of the sky air and clouds.
What thoughts lay edged across
the colours of the rainbow
and the sun's glistening rays.
Maybe a joy that can
be held in the hands
and then let go.

Julie Mears

CHILDHOOD

Children playing outside -
mixing and matching
in the eternal tide of life
as once I did with others
and then the lovers.
How time evaporates,
joins, then separates
my memory of childhood,
its eternity
its uncertainty,
the longing to be adult -
to fly with the wind.
Down through ages cult
what did I find?
Certain happiness -
more or less . . .
But as the children play
I wonder will they
watch and remember
as I do now
the beasts of the night
the nightmares the fright
of one alone on the lone island
of childhood -
loved but misunderstood,
trapped in a dark wood?
I flew. I am here.
They will fly - where?

Gwynneth Curtis

A SENSE OF TASTE

Well, just look at the state of *him*.
He's really *such* a mess.
You'd think he was in pantomime,
from looking at his dress.

And *look*, is that an earring
he's wearing on his nose?
And what's he smeared into his *hair?*
It's chip-fat, I suppose.

His jeans are torn and tattered.
One buttock's hanging out!
I've tried to read his tee-shirt.
God knows what *that's* about!

Is that a *song*, he's singing?
It's just an awful *row*.
It *isn't* one of Tiny Tim's
They can't *write* like that now.

In *my* day, we were trendy.
We kept ourselves so *neat*,
with Jason King moustaches
and platforms on our feet.

With matching shirts and neckties,
we drew admiring stares.
You had to be there, to *believe*
my tank-top and my flares.

The *kids* tore up my caftan.
It's *such* an awful waste.
The trouble with the youth, today;
They have no sense of *taste!*

Lawrence Stewart

THE TRAMP

I must go where the road runs
Like a ribbon beneath the moon,
I must follow the hard-baked earth ruts
On their never-ending turn.

Will I ever see my loved one?
Will we ever meet again?
With the cold night stars within my heart
I walk with the falling rain.

I must go where the hawk flies
Over crag and moor and down,
I must lie on a blanket of bracken,
My head on a pillow of stone.

With my plastic carrier bags
Ever swinging along at my side,
Carrying all my worldly goods,
My lonely despair and pride.

I must go where the frost bites
Where icicles drip from the bough,
Weary feet in their worn boot leather
Making footstep in the white snow.

I must seek the street corners
And sleep in the shop doorway,
And huddle inside cardboard boxes
At the end of each dreary day.

Will I ever see my loved one?
Will we ever meet again
As the cold night stars within my heart
Freeze with the falling rain?

Esme Francis

REGRET

I felt a trembling wonder going down my spine,
When I'd just finished the first bottle of wine,
I remember the week before with my friend, Clare,
We were joking around and she bet a dare.

In despair I take another bottle out of the fridge,
The regrettable dare was to walk on the edge of the bridge,
I double dared her and made her go first,
I know it was the thing you could do worst.

She laughed and danced on the edge an so did I,
I had no idea she would slip and die,
I now mourn her death with liquor in front of me,
For being stupid, for being irresponsible, I plead guilty.

Nahieda Bi

TO A SPECIAL LADY

It's good to have neighbours,
    who are both helpful and kind,
There is a lady called Bunt,
    who springs quickly to mind,
She often provides me,
    with a special scrumptious treat,
For her home baked scones,
    are delectable, delicious to eat,
If I happen to be out,
    when she comes knocking on my door,
I return later to find,
    double wrapped scones waiting for me on the floor,
Pushed through the letter box,
    there to find.
Oh, the pleasure of this treasure,
    truly the very best kind,
How does one thank a good neighbour,
    who is also a friend such as this,
I would like to pay her this tribute,
    Bunt, each bite of your scones, sheer bliss!

Mary Adamson

WHAT WE DESERVE?

When a man has lost his living
and his job has long since gone.
With leaden feet he goes to the DSS,
and the dole he then signs on.
Some people think it's easy money,
but it's barely enough to survive.
And you have plenty of time to contemplate,
if it's even worth you being alive.
With no chance of jobs and no growth industry,
People lose all hope,
and most importantly, their dignity.
Employment isn't a divine right,
just for people with degrees.
Every man and woman deserves the opportunity
to work, to fulfil their needs.
All you politicians,
and power people in high places,
You many work numerical problems out,
but where's the work for all the faces?
Because you don't care about the people
this situation is defeating,
You don't understand the tragedy,
of the mistakes you're still repeating.
Politicians election chant states, *Vote for me*
But what are we voting for?
What we want is jobs,
and that, they all seem to ignore.
We want to work, we need to work,
We deserve our dignity.
Work ensures quality to love our life,
and to love life,
is to be free . . .

Paula Holdstock

THE RAMBLERS

The wind cuts like jagged glass
chilling our blood with its nonchalant torture
And we could be any on this hill today
sad little beasts trailing sad little lives.
Sheep run as promises before us on the path ahead
broken and gone as soon as said and seen
The tussocked grass leaves a lingering sigh
and is joined by the pain of a lustreless Race below.

We tread forever
On past the fossil windmill
through gorse which stabs with a taunt of triumphant simplicity.
Birds seem to shatter like hope under heat
a starling mass of screeching nothing
The sky seems to shake with the terror that we can create
Pitiful souls of a Midas touch.

And the rain comes soft in a grip with dusk
soothing our throats and cementing our husks to the slope.
Flesh in the mists we're consumed by such passion
yet also forlorn we are lost in an alien source
at which we can only tremble.
We blink back the tears and begin the descent
Earth-sucked steps and only the city light to soothe our wistful pallor.

Paul Swaffer

OUR CUSTOMER JACK

Seated on the bar stool
Our customer Jack
In one hand Theakstons Bitter
The other a cigarette pack

Sporting a wiry moustache
Which curls around his face
He will speak to anybody
Or may stare off into space

He fills us with his problems
Almost every day
Everything he confides
Is sad in every way

The melody of Patsy Cline
Echoes through the room
Tears appear in his eyes
Always at this tune

Eight pints of bitter later
And a whisky always neat
His face has flushed a shade of red
And he's quivering in his seat

Always wearing his grey mac
It's never off his back
The bar will lose its character
Without our customer Jack.

Donna Louisa Caldwell

IF ONLY THE ASHES COULD SPEAK...

It was the Russian communists who coined the phrase:
'Man - it sounds proud!' Then put the young ruffians on the trucks
                                                      and set ablaze...
And you? And others? Are they worse? Are they better, or the best?
Of you I am speaking, of you, all men, of the East and the West!
Oh! If the ashes of the past generations could revive...
What details would they not give us about man's
                                                murders and crimes!
In fear and tremor - the hairs on one's head would stand on end;
On hearing the shrieks and screams of the tortured -
                                                one would faint...
What sort of tools of torture did you not invent to your delight?
Aah! You alone, among all the species, do this to your own kind...
On the sight of you - animals and birds tremble, and their
                                                hearts throb;
Some of them entirely disappeared from the face of the globe!
You destroyed them, poor dumb creatures, by your snares,
                                                traps and gun
(You didn't spare even butterflies which danced in the sun...).
It's your hand, in the labs, give them untold suffering and pain...
Why do you transplant two heads to a poor dog, how
                                                would you explain?
Sheer curiosity? Search for the cure of the ills of mankind?
Bah! None of you is so noble - while cruel to animals, unkind;
Humanity - from many of its ills no doubt itself will save
If stops its follies: to smoke, to drink, and practice perverted sex,
Man! Throw off the mask of altruism, and show your true face bare,
It's not high aims, but Nobel Prize, and vanity - that's your affair.
Your obsessions are the three strong MPs: Money, Power, Sex,
To obtain these - you are using all the Machiavellian tricks.
Your cruelty towards everything - is ingrained in your blood,
It's you, lords and kings, used to send out to war young,
                                                unspoiled lads;
You taught them (and still do, mass media through)
                                                to kill, rape, destroy!
An inborn streak runs - the killer and rapist is now a schoolboy!

Fiendish man! You kill your parents, wife, rape your babies -
　　　　　　　　　　　　　　　　　　　　you are insane!
Who can tell, what in my heart prevails - the fear of you or
　　　　　　　　　　　　　　　　　　　　　just disdain . . .

Barbara J Niemienionek-Lindsay

EMPATHY

In the greenhouse we were playing cricket
Bowling insult upon accusation
Smashing the ball without hesitation
Out through the glass into the thicket
To be lost in the undergrowth of pain
Where we searched for our battered love in vain
As it lay hid beneath the peaceful ground
Dormant and so afraid to make a sound
Till the anger in our hearts abated
And we once again appreciated
The kindness and concern that we both felt
Despite the countless trials that life had dealt:
Compose yourself when trouble does arise,
Resentment grows without a compromise.

Paul Hutton

THAT'S LIFE

You go to work - you save and strive
Yo will not shirk - you stay alive
You feign not ill when you are well
You know you will produce and sell

Despite your pace - your spit and grit
Sometimes you know your face won't fit
Your future lurks like blackest night
The bosses shirk - you know you're right

The order book is almost blank
Dark rumours rule - the future's rank
Then comes the day the firm goes bust
There is no pay - and go you must

So what say you of hours hard spent
Your failing view - your back all bent?
Tough luck old friend you try again
CV in hand in wind and rain

For only you can take the buck
and only you will make your luck
There's always space for those who fight
to take their place - make things go right.

I know - for I have passed this way
So don't be shy
Come out to play!

Wilf Lawrence

MOTHER NATURE'S COMPLAINT

'They have stripped my left hand bare,
And my right crumbles, in their grip,
As easily as a gurgling stream flows.
They've gouged my abdomen, they can see my organs.
How I look at my pale, ruined flesh.
How I yearn, beckon, wish
For the rich dark colours of my youth!
They all worshipped my youth;
Every thing was grateful, every body sacrificed.
But now . . .
They strip my back bare.
They strip my strong back bare!'

Martin Forman

WAVES

Blue sky with white clouds,
Hot sandy beaches all around,
White birds fly high in the sky.
How you laughed,
As a wave touched my thigh,
The cold water of the sea,
You were on the shore,
Watching me,
A slight cool breeze began to blow,
And the waves rolled up against
the sandy shore,
As we walked along the shore
holding hands.
Laughing as we went.
Sunset soon came round,
And all we heard was the sound
of the waves beating on the rocks.
And the harbour lights
off the distanced shore.

Rose Hosking

PRICELESS

You'd meet,
If you didn't have this other bloke.
I'm sure of that,
For all your protests
That it has no bearing on us.

I only ask
That I'm allowed one more chance
To look into your face,
To hear your gentle voice,
To touch your soft cheek,
To kiss.

It's not much,
But it would mean a lot.
By denying me even that little I ask
You make it an unattainable target.
You have escalated its worth
To something I can never afford.
Priceless.

Andy Botterill

GREAT EXPECTATIONS

Teeming, great expectations,
Radiant anticipation, afraid, willing, sacrifice reputation,
Irredeemable act, self gratification.
Self induced pain, pleasure, self motivation,
Unknown emotions released self gratification,
Chose to relinquish, sacrificed, lost forever cannot retain.
Passion chosen, over self restraint,
Why allow intellect float far, far away,
Promised passions unforgettable passion filled day.
Irretrievable given to man,
Make absolutely certain, no longer wish to refrain,
Elite no longer can attain what gain.
Relinquished your all,
Words of men many will fall, overcome by all,
Softly spoken words, innocence go unheard,
Gentleness, frailness, softness, sweetness, willingness to please,
Will it appease, desire to need,
Thy gift replenish the earth,
They deeds fulfil mankind's needs.
Many released precious gift.
Without thought, dignity, self respect,
Fear to look back, in humble retrospect.

John Goldsbrough

SAND OF TIME

Has anyone seen footsteps,
In the sand?
They are made by the foot of man,
Where have they come from?
Where will they go?
That is a secret, no one knows.

They disappear for a while,
The sea takes the marks away - made by man and child.

Come back another day,
And we will see,
The marks of time -
Waiting for you and me.

The sea rushes in -
With a roar,
But the footsteps -
Will appear once more.

I have a picture of footsteps in the sand,
They were made by just one man.

B Jones

TEARDROPS

Long after you left and all the heartbreak
I'd sit on the banks by the tranquil lake
Dreaming and wiping the tears from my eyes
Watching stars twinkling in the blue night skies
Lingering there sadly from dusk to dawn
Wondering why you left me alone and forlorn
After you'd gone something inside of me died
You'll never know how many teardrops I cried
Through the dew of my teardrops I see the moon
Hoping my heartaches will be all over soon
I know not when it hurts the worst
Perhaps it's when the bubbles burst
When all my fantasy's and dreams
Have flown on yesterday's winds it seems
The pain and heartache I feel inside
I must face it all: Swallow my pride
Accepting it all in life as a fact
With my soul for the future I'll make a pact
Smile on for tomorrow is another day
Hope in my heart as I go on life's way
Learn: And my mistakes won't be in vain
My heart will mend I'll fall in love again
Carelessly I let you break my heart
Couldn't stay together we had to part
No matter what happens don't you ever forget
The love you planted in my heart lives on yet
Right now my eyes are misty with dew
Of fresh new teardrops I shed for you.

Carol Anne Burnup

THE RAILWAY CHILD

I used to play by the railway line,
Old, disused, worn and decayed;
Amongst the gravel, coke and coal,
Full of dirt and grime, I played.

So happy was I all alone,
In those golden summer days,
The sun obscured by dust and sand,
Making up my childish plays.

I'd skip up to the railway line,
And pretend that I could see
An engine chugging slowly down,
Guard and driver waved to me.

I wonder if I'll ever see
That old railway line again,
Perhaps destroyed now? Never mind,
It served its purpose not in vain.

Mary Hayworth

SILVER RAIN

The day we rode to Ely, love,
the unforbidden rain
came down from Fenland's dreary skies
and damped our hearts in vain.

The day we rode to Ely, love,
you did not make a fuss,
despite your claustrophobia upon the omnibus.

The day we rode to Ely, love,
it was a Sabbath day,
a quarter of a century,
two hundred miles away.

George Pearson

THE SOUNDER

On a concrete walkway towering above town,
Stood a crystal glass man in a shimmering gown.
Rainbow prisms shooting barbs of reflected light,
He shone throughout the day, as he shone throughout night.

People were drawn to him, he listened as they spoke,
He didn't interrupt, with a comment or joke.
They feared the silences and talked their lives away,
They spewed their histories year by year, day by day.

They could see right through him, they thought he did likewise.
Without word of reply, he forced them to summise.
Each gave a synopsis of their expected fate,
But he made no judgement, no outcome would he state.

Some of them went away to commit suicide,
Others took their exit with arrogance and pride.
Some of them felt they'd been justified to the hilt,
Others were pondering a profound sense of guilt.

They had sealed their own fates they'd been their own counsel,
They had made their heavens and they had made their hell.
And the crystal glass man moved to another town,
A sounding board need wear neither a smile or frown.

John Noble

THE FLOWER SHOW

The flowers on the border were waiting for the match
Small ones on the front and tall ones at the back.

All the bees and butterflies were putting on a show
Taking all the pollen out and flying to and fro.

The flowers were all laughing at every joke they cracked.
The small ones at the front and the tall ones at the back.

Now the Show was almost over, and the butterflies and bees,
Seem to bow to all the flowers as each one takes his leave.

The flowers close their petals as in a way they clap,
The small ones in the front and the tall ones at the back.

V N King

IN MY ATTIC

So many lost treasures to be found
Of my life so richly bound,
Some, of simple easy leisure
Have given many hours of pleasure.

Old photograph albums covered in dust
A first bicycle now going to rust,
The cradle in which my young were rocked
Love letters in a chest, safely locked.

School reports neatly placed aside
The hobby horse we'd wildly ride!
Two little costumes of Halloween witches
Multi-coloured scarf, many dropped stitches!

Odd scraps remain of a party dress
My first attempt, I remember the mess!
Trinkets, love tokens, a poetry book
Teenage photograph, of the sixties look!

There are more secrets hiding here
All of them so simple yet, dear,
My Aladdins' cave of memories and magic
Reliving yesterday, in my dusty, old attic.

Sue Jackson

DIRECTIONAL THOUGHTS

A lonely figure, a tiny speck to someone's eye,
Long stretches of rock that often meet the sky,
Older than me, it sees all of the changes,
Never changing position, its view often ranges.

Envelopes of cloud often caress the mountain peak,
On this day no clouds, the winds must be weak,
Nothing to believe in, just a world full of lies,
And the silence is broken as a hunting buzzard cries.

Mountains blend together, they are rarely alone,
On the other hand, humans are often made of stone,
Unemployment is evil, a body that has no soul,
No human being should have to survive on the dole.

The jobless person is no lesser person, so don't hide,
As a drone waits to die, completely stripped of pride,
Inundated with time, all I do is poison my mind,
North winds hound me, with the past I left behind.

Looking at the sun, squinted eyes, face in knots,
On closing my eyes there are a thousand coloured dots,
Overtaken by altitude, I laid back in a dream,
Kaleidoscopic colours spin, my mind and body scream.

In the distance to the left, western unchartered land,
Nearer, but still distant, to my right the sea and sand,
Gone from behind me, my mind blocks out the north,
South lies my future, yet another long lonely rebirth.

Opening my eyes, once again reality starts to dawn,
Under the spell of sleep, it is evening, no longer morn,
Taken from the womb where we were safe with no pain,
Hurt by many years of being left out in the rain . . .

A Bacon

THE FACTORY WORKER

I don't want to be here, doing this, I have no choice
Oh to escape, a mind-break for sanity's sake, I feel like dying
Seeing as a stranger a visitor, I hear far off, my own voice
Talking, responding, smiling and yet, I feel like crying

Time to slip out, visit a magnetic landscape, an inner space
Time ceases to taunt me as I slip headphones over my ears, now
Time stands still, outside fades, mind enters another place
Time is meaningless, hands still working out there, somehow

Now swirling, falling, sinking into the eye of the storm
Now calming, refreshing, moving music bathing my mind
Questions, answers, opinions ideas, replace my worker's yawn
Now memories places, feelings faces, unfolding as I unwind

Brain recharging, nourishing on new thoughts, and knowing
Body on auto-pilot, knows what to do without me to supervise
Imagination flowing, colours glowing, frustration going
My inner voice sings for me alone to hear, no one to criticise

Nearly time for a coffee-break, maybe treat myself to a cake
Believe I can face reality again, feeling stronger
Ready to leave my secret world, and return to the parts I make
Wonderful, an hour has rushed by and I'm depressed no longer.

David Kennedy

A MOMENT IN ETERNITY

A moment in eternity
A moment in your love
Words which pledge our destiny etched within my heart
Love marries our devotion
Two hearts within one soul
Two lovers walk together, thus a promise lights the dark

You are my Jerusalem
The Altar of my dream
Venus is your heart, while my love is in your soul
I reach beyond a fantasy and kiss your sensuous smile
And caught the vows we promised before the moment grew too old

Love shall be our honeymoon
Blessed in Camelot
Our dreams baptised by heaven in immortalised belief
My Guinevere is waiting
My Juliet of love
In her heart our world is captured though the journey maybe brief

Capri's our morning paradise
Rome's our eternal night
The Rhine's the afternoon we choose to appreciate our life
Our candle shined on Venice, we sailed its rippled streets
Embraced the limpid centuries where romantic hearts should meet

We touch the eternal moment
And together we will walk
Through the eyes of tomorrow, into the romance of a dove
Scribe's have wrote my testament
The words belong to you
A moment in eternity is a lifetime in your love.

David Bridgewater

CHANGING FACE OF NATURE

On a rustic little coastline,
Rocks are scattered free,
The different shapes and sizes,
Have been moulded by the sea.

The constant weather beating,
And the waves' strength and force,
Has changed this rock formation,
Over several years, of course.

The wind has also damaged,
These rocks that have been changed,
But the sea has caused this sculpture,
To be completely re-arranged.

The sea is never happy,
Its destruction won't decrease,
The waves will keep on coming,
Reluctant to ever cease.

In a hundred years from now,
This scene will change again,
Once more the sea will be at fault,
It's nature, I can't explain.

Sarah Maycock

THE SCOTTISH CUP FINAL - 1994

The whole of Dundee is really excited
After the triumph of Dundee United,
Now the Hampden hoodoo is over and done
For the Scottish Cup brave United have won,
Yes they went to Hampden knowing the dangers
And managed to beat The Glasgow Rangers,
Now down Ibrox way they are quiet and still
'Cos they were defeated by one goal to nil,
At the half-time whistle there was no scoring
But no one could say that the game was boring,
Then after the restart a United booster
For they got a goal scored by Craig Brewster,
And that was the goal that won them the cup
Let's hope that United are now on the up,
And maybe this will be just the beginning
Of many more trophies they will be winning.

David Wilson

OUR LITTLE PIECE OF HEAVEN

You're all so different!
The gentle scholar and the quiet thinker;
That naughty tinker with mud upon his clothes and cheeky grin;
Our red-haired agitator,
Fiery instigator of fiercesome but friendly fights;
The gruff-voiced, blonde teenager,
Clever though, still,
Somehow it's just on schooldays he's ever ill.

Five precious gifts from God,
Loaned to us, not given;
Troublesome at times
But, nonetheless, our little piece of heaven.

Rosemary Thomson

THE WORLD THROUGH A LITTLE BOY'S EYES

There's a little room I visit in the back of my mind,
I was given a map, so now it's easy to find.
When I went through the door for the very first time,
I blew away the dust and it started to shine.
I wondered to myself how long could it last,
Then I realised I'd stumbled on my childhood past.
And that there's one thing to help me, seek truth from lies,
That's to look at the world through a little boys eyes

I left my old room with the key in my pocket,
Now I keep it inside of a heart shaped locket.
I promised myself, that I would return there,
When I had a problem that I needed to share.
When I'm faced with a battle, where I must fight evil,
I search through this room to find something that's equal.
When I need to find something to help me survive,
I'll look at the world through a little boy's eyes.

What I'm trying to say, is that everyone has one,
Life can be hard, so we all need to have fun.
Our skin may get wrinkled, our hair might all fall out,
But there'll always be memories floating about.
We may leave time, but time never leaves us,
At the end of the road we can still catch the school bus.
Playing with toy guns is not just for children,
If you play with fire, it's you who will get burnt.
So if I want to be happy, before I die,
Again I'll look at the world from a little boy's eyes.

Chris Hamlin

REFLECTIONS

There he is at the end of the pier
drifting away on stormy waters
A north sea wind restores the dying spirit
forever peering outside in and just not with it

A nightly stroll beneath the lights will ease a troubled mind
But if you have not got one now you never will
the sounds of the soft easy sea brings it back to me
And to this day those unforgettable words haunt him still

By means of narrow sea-front streets
the chosen route to his temporary home
What does the future hold what lays ahead
it is the same old story to return alone.

I rise into a new day and the sun is shining
The gulls shout in a blue cloudless sky
And with the ocean being its usual noisy self
this truly is much more than just a seaside town.

David Cooper

HARDSHIP BUILDS CHARACTER - BUT LONELINESS BUILDS WALLS

January, February, the months role on, but am I getting any wiser?
Experience after experience, life takes its toll;
hardship builds character but loneliness builds walls.
Mistrust replaces misplaced trusts, suspicion old loves torn.
The average person learns to trust that no one trusts at all.

Rosalyn Carr

THE HEDGE

It's an ever changing scene,
Yet it remains the same,
To the farmer it's a windbreak,
To the fledgling it's a game.

In the garden it's seclusion
From sharp and prying eyes
Escept the chopper pilots
Passing in the skies.

There's insects, berries, grubs and nuts,
Among its fabric closely wound,
To feed the birds and animals
That flourish on the ground.

In the winter it's their shelter
In the summer it's their shade
It's their home, their world, their refuge
That only Nature made.

Peggy Love

THE FOAMING SEA

The wind is strong and gusting storm,
Its anger plainly seen.
Bows crash down through foaming white
To hide in darkest green.
Fearsome waves form overhead,
Then crash with searching sea.
Tearing anchors from their chains,
Setting shackles free.
Ropes pulled tight as music string
Sing an eerie wail.
Masts are loud in agony,
Tormented by their sail.
A sudden crack is heard by all
As topmast starts to fly.
It hovers like an angel child
Then soars into the sky.
Thunder crash and lightening flash
Alight the sky with flame.
The brave stand fast upon the deck
As others hide in shame.

Alan Mitchell

CALEDONIAN ISLES

They have built the new ferry
With comfort in mind,
The plush carpets and seats
Are passenger-kind

With a rest for your elbows
And a cover for your head,
To convince early travellers
They are back in their bed.

But as for the view
Of Brodick's curved strand,
Sheltered by Claughlands
And rocky Merkland,

The seats are too low,
Or the windows too high,
So when you sit down
All you see is the sky.

Richard Stewart

THURSDAY NIGHTS

Outstretched feline like across the floor,
Finger-licking,
Dipping into life.

Melting like a Carmen or Lolita,
Planned liaisons in lace top stockings,
Brief encounters, too short-lived.

I feel safe with my friends,
Moments spent spilling out secrets;
exciting and thrilling.
Sharing satisfaction,
Safer than sex,
Dependable, durable,
Delicious Thursday Nights.

Cath Cunningham

WILLOW

The old willow
by the River Darent
has gone. Cantilevered
across my early memories;
pollarded, gnarled
into Rackhamesque contortions;

it bore our young weight
as we sat, with eddied fronds
of green beneath our feet.

Idly dangling predictions
of the future, voyages
through an uncharted world;

our thoughts
were sprays of elder flower:
we tossed them in the flow,
watched their sodden lace
recede through fields
of drifting buttercups,
always trusting
they would reach the sea.

John Arnold

A STUDENT'S LAMENT

At eighteen you *know it all* and can't wait to get away
To college miles from home, although your parents want you to stay.
At first it's exciting, new friends made, new places to go.
Student Unions, Nightclubs, you begin to love it so.
But you soon realise being a student is not all honey
You sometimes feel lonely, and never have enough money.
As the weeks pass your grant begins to disappear
And you wonder how you'll manage to make it last a year.
So you go back home for a few days and live in luxury
Hot baths, clean clothes and eat breakfast, dinner and tea!
You return to college refreshed, and soon get back in the swing
Of student life and all the freedom it does bring.
But you know you can go home whenever you feel like a break
And be welcomed back, and your laundry you can take.
So although you're independent, you realise that you
Are lucky you've a nice family to keep returning to.
When you get your Degree, it will all have been worthwhile
And your parents will be there, wearing the biggest smile.

Barbara Wheatley

WITH LOVE EACH DAY

Each day I promise not to try to solve all my life's problems,
At once or alone,
Nor shall I expect you to resolve them either,
You have troubles enough of your own,
Each day I promise to communicate my joy as well as my sorrow,
So that we can know each other better, now and tomorrow.

Each day I promise to remind myself that I am an imperfect
human being,
And never demand perfection from you at any rate,
Until I myself am perfect, so you see you are safe!
Each day I promise myself, never to step inside your head,
With my soiled feet,
Many of us are guilty of this action, but most of us never realise it,
We are far too busy seeking self-satisfaction.

Each day I promise to try to learn something new,
About you and me and the world we live in,
So that I can continue to experience all things, as if they are
newly born,
At the same time allowing you to think entirely free,
Not to be imprisoned by a mind forlorn, or worse still by me.

Each day I promise to really listen and to hear your point of view,
To discover the least threatening way of presenting mine,
Remembering that we are both growing and changing,
In a hundred different ways, with the passage of time and the days.

Each day I promise to reach out and touch you gently,
If not with my hands, through the medium of my mind,
Because I do not want to miss experiencing you,
And the uniqueness of our time,
Each day I promise to dedicate myself again,
To the continual process of loving you with infinite care,
As all we have on this earth is temporary,
There are no certainties for tomorrows,
Tomorrow may not be there.

Each day I promise and sincerely pray,
As we walk together along life's way,
If I cannot love you, let me not hurt you in any way.

Shirley Boyson

THE CLOWN

At the little village circus
Where children throng
To find their joy,
The place where sorrow
Is momentarily laid aside,
Lives the loneliest clown.

Here, where people crowd
To venture into another world
Of entertainment, colour and laughter,
To see the thin man
With the permanent painted smile
Behind which his forlorn state is hidden;

The place where one
Cannot hear himself think,
Where music deafens the listener
Drowning the true nature of life,
Intoxicating the mind,
Where fear cannot prevail;

Where the scene upon the stage
Seems all merry and gay;
But alas were the spectator
To gaze deep inside
The eyes of the clown
His laughter would cease and die.

Here where his destiny lies
His troubles unsolved
And none to care,
This man with the radiant smile
Grows weaker and weaker every day
While we drink from the fountain of his life.

Raymond Fenech

SUNSET

How I love to watch the sunset, with its iridescent light,
Watching the clever way that it changes day to night,
Going from the lightness, to a dusky pink,
As into the sea, the sun appears to sink,
Then when the darkness creeps, all across land and sea,
'Tis then that I must go, for home's the place to be.

L Smith-Warren

A BRAVE FACE

Room strewn with clutter,
dark and cold,
face hewn with worry,
prematurely old.

Smile tinged with sadness,
touch of sorrow,
eyes ringed with shadows,
dream of tomorrow.

Harsh task of living,
kept at bay,
fresh mask of make up,
meet the new day.

Austere, bleak world,
hope is faint,
lost lady shelters,
behind powder and paint.

Michael Webb

LOOK UP

Can't you lift your eyes up once,
    Just once and look around?
See just what is going on,
    Not there upon the ground.

People's houses smashed and torn,
    Old folks black and blue.
Women raped, children abused,
    What are we to do?

Is prison the answer, or the birch,
    Should we bring back the rope?
There must be some thing we can do,
    We've got to have some hope.

It's not just deterrent that we want,
    It's action that we lack.
The ones that do these dreadful things,
    Should always feel pain back.

So lift your eyes up off the ground,
    Just once and have a look.
People don't care any more,
    About the rules in life's great book.

A B Hughes

THE GREATEST GAME?

They regard it as a northern sport,
Now you southerners just take heed
The greatest sport with the greatest bums -
Yes, it's rugby league.

Before you turn your noses up,
Please listen to my claim
That the greatest legs and the muscliest pecs
Are found in this great game.

Watching every Sunday
The G-strings and tight shorts -
Their rippling thighs of tree trunk size
Are always in my thoughts.

But what about the rugby?
Well, it's all just scoring tries
It's the thirteen men that are doing it
That are dreamy on the eyes!

Plenty of girls and women
Feel just the way I do,
See Alan Hunte and Andy Platt
And you would see it too.

So come on all you softies
These guys need some kissin'
And come up to the north of the land
And see what Gods you're missin'!

Carol Spellman (17)

GLIDING TO WHAT SHOULD HAVE BEEN

Take me up, set me free
Leaving this crumbling world behind
Touch the sky, feel the sun
Know every tangled thought unwind.

Smell the air, hear the wind
Feel the peace and watch the heartache
Fall away, gone forever
Just contentment in its wake.

Green and gold, blue and silver
My eyes won't believe this splendour
A world so different
So much beauty, so full and tender.

To soar above and beyond the clouds
Man has built this machine
Graceful, fragile, a thing of beauty
Man has dreamt of what should have been.

So take me up, set me free
To touch eternity, more to believe
In beauty, in liberty
In our last chance for reprieve.

Gill Oliver

THE GIRLS' NIGHT OUT

Every week in the Rose and Crown
The girls come in then go up town
There's Sharon, Nic, Leigh and Deb too
We have one drink then need the loo.

We aim to get drunk each night we're out
Nicola and Leigh do without a doubt
But Sharon and Deb no matter how hard they try
They can never seem to get very high.

We all enjoy the bus ride a lot
The only problem is it's not at all hot
We sing our songs and kneel on our knees
But Mr Bus Driver, don't throw us off, please.

We get in Kipps' and need the loo
Then from the bar get a drink or two!
We dance around and sing to Wham!
And Abba, The Specials and Duran Duran.

When the night has ended we get some food
Then it's 3 o'clock by the time we've walked and queued
We share a taxi back to Leigh's
Then we climb into bed and go to sleep with ease.

Sharon Utting

IN MY SPARE TIME ...

Just a moment of time,
Of an awakening to nature,
Of dreams, seasons gone,
And the welcome of summer,
As sun-kissed flowers burst in bloom,
Of laughter, hope is to wonder,
Upon my feet a bed of cool crisp clover,
In the distances, shadows peeping through,
Skies so ever blue on a magical gleam,
Sparkling water such beauty of a thousand eyes,
As day is to night,
Sunlight, moonlight,
Stir within me,
This the beginning,
A moment ...

Paula E O'Connor

OUT AGAIN

Tonight's the night to get it right,
I'm going out again.
I'll spend an hour getting dressed,
In the hope of meeting men.
When I arrive I scan the room,
And focus on my prey;
He's standing there at the bar,
I know he's mine today.
As I go up to make my claim
I see him look at me.
He's happy now and smiling,
But it's his girlfriend's face he sees.
I walk away so disappointed,
Ready to go home,
But then I see my friends around me
And know I'm not alone.

Dominique Woolf

MY THEATRE TREAT

An evening at the theatre,
Always leaves me feeling right.
Relaxing in a comfy seat,
I'm settled for the night.

I've bought myself a programme
To see who plays which part,
Curtains open, lights are dimmed
We are ready for the start.

My chocolate sweets are melting,
I'll have to eat them quickly.
It's now the half-time interval,
My tummy's feeling sickly.

Here comes the ice-cream lady,
With my lolly on a stick.
A bag of crisps, some nuts to chew,
I'm going to be sick.

A visit to the ladies,
To freshen up and then.
A gin and tonic on the way
To watch the play again.

The final curtain closes,
Just one thing left to do.
A frantic search beneath my seat,
Help, someone's moved my shoe.

I stumble in a taxi,
To shelter from the rain.
Next week I'll be coming back
To do it all again.

P E Taylor

A COMPLETE KNIT!

It's one of the oldest yarns in my book,
The story of just how long it took
With Mum to guide me
(More like, deride me)
In my pathetic attempts with crochet and hook.

Let's try something simpler, she said in a fit.
The staggeringly easiest *Easi-Knit*.
It won't take long,
But I proved her wrong -
In three years I still haven't finished it.

I would like to say that I followed the pattern,
But Physics and Chemistry elude this slattern.
Dec? Purl? and Inc?
Brought me to the brink
Of tears, as I struggled with unwieldy batons.

I daydreamed about the pride I would feel
If I was wrapped in my home-made Chenille.
This spurred me on,
Knit one, Purl one,
Till my fingers and thumbs were a mass of weals.

I carefully checked the garment I'm making,
When filled with horror, 'less I'm much mistaken,
I purled the wrong side,
And just sat and cried
At the miserable chaos that I've been creating.

I hurled it aside, and brought down the gavel,
To show it was finally time to unravel
This mass of spaghetti,
Concede, and forget it,
And stick to a gentler pursuit - like space travel!

Claire Morgan

CITY MOON

I can't compare you to the autumn
when the colours are bleached by morning fogs
and every winter there are icicles
at the entrance of the Underground
While the spring whispers in my ear
like the lap of a butterfly wing
It is only summer when I wake to see
the sun almost as bright as your smile
that it teaches torches to burn bright.

I lie on my back at midnight
and all I can give you's a city moon
to chain your wishes to.

Ian Duckett

THE BEAUTY BATTLE

It's Saturday night and the bathroom door's locked
On the inside I stand, staring at the mirror in shock!
I have bags under my eyes that Sainsbury's could use
And my hair is all tangled, it'll never diffuse.

I glance at my watch and see the seconds tick by
As I grab chunks of hair, I let out a cry!
I'm armed with several lotions and a full tube of gel
But I've only got two hours to create the look of au naturel!

I quickly shower and shampoo and I wax and I shave
Only to be confronted with a head of hair that just won't behave
So I attack it with tongs, hot brushes, rollers that are heated
                                                                             and velcro
A can of mousse and hairspray later and I'm nearly ready to go!

But to my horror of horrors another dilemma lies ahead
Do I choose hotpants or flares - perhaps lycra instead?
The lycra it is - to hide my spare tyre and bulge
Memories of lunchtime and fudge cake that I shouldn't have indulged.

In two hours I've created a look resembling perfection
I could be mistaken for Ms Schiffer with this flawless complexion!
The final addition, a pair of platforms for my feet
Then a gleeful glance in the mirror at my look that's now complete!

Sarah Robinson

TIME TO SPARE

Somewhere to sit in the sunshine, that's what I'd love
Somewhere to rest and be thankful, a blue sky above
Feeling the warmth on my face, like a loving caress
Bathed in the bliss of the moment, purring with happiness
A seat in a park or a garden or in a street or square
It would be heaven or something quite near it
A personal blessing it seems
To bask in the glow and glory along with my thoughts and dreams
Or having a word with a stranger
A quiet impersonal chat. Discussing the whims of the weather
Talking of this and that.
That's all I want when work is finished and desires fade away.
Enjoying the end of the day.

There is much to be said for a place in the sun
Where cares seem to float away.
No worries, no sorrow just laughter and fun
From morning until close of the day.

Mary Stirling

TIME OF MY OWN

What do I do when I've time to spare?
Not a lot, the occasion's so rare.
But if I had, I might go away,
All alone by myself for a day.
I'd get up early at break of dawn
To face the elements I'd wrap up warm,
Stealthily, silent I'd roll down the lane
Prying eyes can be such a pain.
Out on the road I'd put on the power
Bending slightly, like breeze on a flower,
Gathering speed, wind on my cheeks
Climbing steadily up towards the peaks.
Alone at last, no-one can chide
No-one to say I'm too old to ride
This great big beautiful motor bike,
Much more fun than a boring hike.
If my family could see me in my kit
They'd throw up their arms and have a fit,
They'd say they hadn't seen the like
Of their granny cavorting on a bike.
One of these days I'll shock the lot,
Then, I'll be happy, if they are not.

Margaret Laws

FRIENDS

Huddling now together, a circle we do form,
As we meet in the corridor just outside my dorm.
We sit and share our stories, our happiness and pain,
From each other's experience, we certainly have now gained.

Often you may find us, sitting in one room,
Discussing life and nature, and ever approaching doom.
We may reveal our heart, to every one and all,
Knowing that our secrets, will not go out this wall.

So we help each other out, in many many ways,
Here to comfort and console, on happy and sad days.
But soon our time will be up, each will take a lane,
And I'll assure you now, that we will meet again.

Nuala Fitzpatrick

QUALITY LEISURE

Walking along the pristine golden sands
smoothed by God with loving, caring hands.
The tide has just gone out
the world seems newly born
No-one is about
My footprints only, can be clearly seen
as though a human being had never been.
God's giant duster wiping earth's slate clean.

Seabirds wheeling, diving, soaring, crying,
whipped by the breeze, the calls of freedom dying
while my labrador bounds past.
Ears flapping - heart pounding - legs flying
free at last.
Spangled droplets sparkling by the sea
as she showers them to the sky with glee
ecstatic in her leisure time with me.

God threw the moon into the sky, so will it see
mirrored in the ebb and flow, life's ups and downs to be
I feel God's presence near
giving love of life - of health - of hope
of all most dear.
With heedless, careless joy, the dog renewed
her shaking - and water all around me strewed.
While I stood still - felt cleansed, revived, imbued.

V Buchan

THINGS WE GET UP TO

We're just a bunch of ladies who like to have a natter,
Sometimes our charming speakers can't be heard above the chatter,
We've made pretty paper roses and other things so nice,
And we're experts at identifying beetles, bugs and lice.
We've dabbled in astrology, antiques we can evaluate,
Our houses are impregnable, security inviolate.
Our plants grow with abandon, our fingers are so green,
And of course our flower arrangements are something to be seen,
Bingo, bring-and-buy and beetle drives never, ever bore us,
We've had a go at yoga, even tried to sing in chorus,
Sometimes a make-up session leaves us looking rather glamorous,
(Though we're getting rather long in't tooth for assignations
                                                                          amorous),
There've been educational excursions to places far and near,
To conferences and castles - then stopped off for a beer!
We've called at garden centres, had many tasty teas,
Our numerous activities should bring us to our knees,
May our guild go on for ever bringing happiness and pleasure,
So come along and join us for an hour or two of leisure.

J Melling

THE BOOTFAIR PUNTER

I always have plenty of time to spare
For my favourite pastime a Boot Fair
I'm wide awake at the crack of dawn
Without so much as a groan or a yawn
I leap out of bed and peer through the pane
Please, oh please, don't let it rain
Are you sure that it's here, have you got the right date
Of course I am silly, hurry we're late
Now that we've parked, I'll just have a nap
Your going to walk right through that cow clap
There's lots of cars, I'm now on a high
In anticipation of what I might buy
Here's the first one, I'll just have a sniffty
If you want any bargains you have to be niffty
I'm looking for Doulton Wedgewood or Crown
No it's not what I thought, I'll just put it down
Dresden or silver or Beswick or Spode
Perhaps I'll find something to wear a la mode
What's that there, oh that's a nice plate
You weren't quick enough, I've just bought it mate
I'm now loaded down with two heavy bags
Serenely oblivious of my aching legs
I've managed to find an old china mug
And I'm ever so pleased with my Claris Cliffe jug
My problem now is to locate the van
Not to mention having to arouse my old man
I hope when I find him he won't start to mock
I don't think he will, when he sees what I've got.

Joan Sharrocks

JUST ANOTHER DAY

'Get back down in that cellar Jacko me lad! Else it'll be grief you see,
No good trying to kid one who's kidded thousands, not one like me!'
'But Bet love it's a dead cert, *Jack the Lad,* at Aintree, you'll see.'
Poor Jack his specs all stuck wi' tape, his brass down t' drain,
                                                                  looks sad,
Perhaps Betty's hotpot will cheer him? Make up for t'bad luck
                                                                      he's had?
Derek with his half of bitter is whining, whimpering, as usual
                                                                    all forlorn,
His venture to be salesman of the year, from Mavis words of scorn!
Old soldier Percy wants proper custard with his treacle pud!
Says he won't go to Spain when he weds Maud, he'll miss his
                                                  roast beef, Yorkshire puds!
'I'd show 'em how to eat proper, to cook jam roly poly, how to
                                                                   mash spuds!'
Could love be in the air for Ken Barlow? How many times will
                                                                      this be?
He's never forgiven Mike Baldwin the spiv! For enticing away
                                                                  his Dierdre.
The cafe's full day or night, baked beans, chips, enough for t'army!
If Alma mortgages it all for love, I think she must be barmy!
Raquel bless her cotton socks, ever hopeful trusting lover boy Des,
Longs to be a cover girl, hit the big time, *she'll never make it!*
                                                                      who sez?
Emily's to wed the vicar! Well she knows he's not exactly
                                                               Clark Gable,
But she'll be able to do as she likes without Percy reorganising
                                                                       if able!
Will Reggie outsmart his ma-in-law, that dreaded lady Mrs Grimes?
You can't teach an old dog new tricks lad! You've tried
                                                                umpteen times!
Betterbuys and Curly, will he find true love, promotion? Oh
                                                              and Vera!
She longs to *tick up,* dreams of little Tommy living nearer.

So now the towels are on the pumps, it's *time gentlemen please!*
We'll close the doors on the Rovers Return, public house extrodinaire,
Just another day with ordinary folk who could live, anywhere!

Joyce M Hefti-Whitney

NEIGHBOURS

At 5.30 everybody sits down
clean or dirty to watch Neighbours.
Everybody's friends in their neighbourhood
everybody is understood.
Neighbours is very exciting
and sometimes very frightening.
They don't get bored but never lonely
and hardly ever seem to get moany.
All Brad ever thinks about is food like burgers 'n' lamb
and Pam has to cook it all.
There's Philip who's good
but Julie sometimes is not understood.
There's Annalise who spreads things and can be bad
while Russell is going mad.
I'm glad my life isn't so busy
otherwise I'd just be tired and dizzy.

Corinne Patty (10)

ANON

Where has it gone - all that hope I'd grown -
Those mapped-out dreams and colour schemes.
My children are here, the seeds are sown
Into pigeon holes and teams.

The school gate's temporary repose
Will soon leave me astray and disposed.
Silly old mum with all those woes -
No certificates, just another chapter closed.

A mother's lot's not a happy one
Only discovered till you're going and gone.
Down you go, blinkered and drained of fun
So they can flourish and leave you *anon*.

Trudie Gordon

INSIDE OUT

All I have to offer you is my love and my trust,
I know it is love, and not just lust.
I watch you and I feel an ache inside,
I can feel you inside me, and you're so alive.
I thought meeting you would make me glad,
But I know it's only making me sad.
I reach out for you, but you're not there
I just lie here and dream, I stand and stare.
You are the man I want, I need,
If only you knew my aching heart would bleed.
As I see your picture in a frame,
I know it's not you I should blame,
If only you could feel the same.
I feel your bodyheat as you walk by,
If only you knew I lie here and cry.
I'm not asking for sympathy,
Just one day that you notice me.
My heart skips, misses a beat,
As I dream of your bodyheat.
I can't control myself any longer,
I'm getting weak, not any stronger.
I want to love you very much,
I want to be your every touch.
I'll collapse and die one day,
And all my dreams will fade away.
I'll be an angel, in heaven above,
I'll be with love, i.e. the dove.

Claire Hart

THE HAND THAT CONTROLS YOU

He sits in a crowd sharing their jokes,
Laughing with them as they demean others,
To purify themselves.
I watch you.
You might as well be alone because your sadness draws me.
Your face is twisted by unsolved pieces of your life.
Each time you raise your glass to quench your hurt,
A cynical smile shows on your lips.
You try to escape it all.
You stay here to avoid home when you are alone.
Left with your own thoughts in case they send you mad.
You realise you are not in control.
People have come and gone,
Because of your need to drink in solitude of mind.
You want to reach out for help,
But fear made the glass your companion.
It no longer eases your pain.
You want the upper hand,
But won't accept help,
Owe anyone or be let down.
You won't stop,
You've been alone too long.
You hate yourself now,
Because you will not change,
You can't on your own.
So you have resigned yourself to being controlled.
I've watched you and though we never speak,
I see you changing.
I wonder why those beside you do not notice,
They too drink to numb truths.
That is why you surround yourself by them.
I'd love to pull up a chair and say to you,
'Drink of my love for life',
But you don't see me,
Only the bottom of your glass.

Rachel Oliver

SPARE TIME

I'm asked of what I do
During my spare time
I like to write a verse or two
Of poetry and rhyme

Many things are written of
But most of all my thoughts
To help me cope with everyday
Life and words; all sorts

Perhaps one day I'll be lucky
And see my name in lights
For my poetry will be published
I will have reached new heights

But I think that for the meantime
I'll try the competition in *Me*
Maybe I'll win three hundred pounds
And be included in Glenn's Anthology.

D E Roderick

VICTIM OF ADDICTION

howl at the moon
you lurkers of night,
creeping round darkness
in some shadowy plight
your devious figure lurks
in the night out on the street
where all lurkers meet

playing with trickery
quiet and sleek
playing your games
on cold empty streets
do you feel like a spring
that hasn't been sprung
do you feel like a clown
whose life has no fun

you're all alone on this
midweek night
cold hungry no friends
in sight
you fell into life's lonesome pit
go find the bag man and
scrounge a hit

howl at the moon you
lurkers of night
play in the darkness
stay out of the light
you're a victim of addiction
in a circle of hate
better set out now before it's
too late.

Russell Dandy

JOSHUA

He was a child of love,
Dreamt up by God above,
Bodies had entwined,
To multiply mankind.

Although they were so young,
His life should have begun,
They could not make it last,
So the infant had to pass.

But still his spirit's there,
Floating in the air,
Bringing pain for her at night,
And to his father - at her sight.

The love they have and care,
Should stop this life's despair,
But secrets cut insides,
Making us speak lies.

Come, let your parents grow,
Your memory will not go,
For she and he are meant to be,
Anyone can see.

Young child go to your rest,
And return when times are best,
One day you'll be born for real,
And tell them of your ordeal.

Fiona Gibb

MAN-KIND

She is a candidate sitting in a waiting room,
Everyone there is full of gloom and doom.

One by one in they called,
Here they'll be assessed, ripped apart and mauled.

Qualifications, potential is all that matters,
By the end of the ordeal your mind is in tatters.

She enters alone with her files clutched to her side,
Wishing she could go home and hide.

The boss looks up and gives her a stare,
And then he pretends she is not there.

She lays down her qualifications upon the table,
But *he* has already decided *she* is not able.

Going for a job which she is refused again,
For she is alone in a world full of men.

Joyeeta Mukherjee

ABANDON SHIP

When I set out, the sea was calm, beneath a gentle breeze
A rhythmic stroke with untied arms, propelled the boat with ease.
The sky turned grey with big black clouds, the sea became
                                        much rougher
Yet still I thought that I could win - but the going was now tougher.
I tossed and rolled on every wave, no headway could I make
I started up my *seagull* motor and soon found my mistake.
It got me to the open seaway, the petrol then gave out
I could not row against the wind - no help was there about.
A sudden fear tore through my mind, I should be lost forever,
Another death claimed by the seas due to changing weather.
Now tears poured down my frightened face, I could not see ahead
I was so cold and shivering wet, my hands a bluey red.
The shoreline rocks with jagged peaks smashed the waves apart.
Frothing death like rabid dog was pounding in their heart.
Not all my desperate efforts could avoid that fate.
The boat struck rock before I knew my efforts came too late.
The froth engulfed and then departed, the boat struck rock
                                        once more,
Then juddered down, to rise again, against that rugged shore.

A windblown call came to my ears, a boy stood on the beach.
He clambered down the rocks to help; my boat still out of reach.
He waded out and caught my bow as the boat rushed forwards
And as the waves came rolling in, slowly pulled me shorewards.
The boy clung on as I got out; together then, we beached it.
Now all was safe upon the sand, relieved, I then just left it!
I went back to fetch it later, the sea once more, was calm.
Despite its looks, I went prepared, that could do no harm.

Elizabeth Melvin

A PRAYER TO GOD

I don't know where I'm going
I've forgotten where I've been
I feel like I've walked round and round
inside this world of sin

My world is getting worse
every single breath I take
but no matter what I say or do
this world's not mine to break

'Cause if I could, I'd start again
and I'd make more good than bad
I would make someone like me
be proud of this world not sad

I'd cry for joy instead of hurt
and I'd make everybody free
not free of the law or government
but free of being like me

If there is a god up there
I pray to him on my knees
help this world and start again
I'm begging you lord, please.

Fiona Donocik (14)

SUNDAY AT THE PIPER

The Piper club on Sunday is never to be missed
The perfect end to a weekend, a last chance to get pissed
Through the doors at midday a table chosen with care
Arrive any later and an empty seat is rare

Browsing through the tabloids with pint and fag in hand
'Put your left hand to your right for the club's resident band!'
Two old boys take the stage namely John and Len
Anticipation fills the air especially from the men

For any moment the lights will dim and in naked glory we'll see
'The body-beautiful for your delight - it's the lovely Cindy Lee!'
Cabaret artiste follows on, trousers always tight
He sings the songs your mother should know
From this there's no respite

A final rush for bingo, minutes before eyes-down
Twenty quid to play for so *ssh!* not a sound
Raffle prize is up for grabs, a frozen joint of beef
The winning number's drawn and called
The compere's wife is on her feet

Have a go at talent spot, a free pint if you dare
Frank Sinatra and Jennifer Rush are the usual standard fare
Local folk and students make up the rowdy crowd
There's always a few of the latter who carry on too loud

Political correctness - it's not the club's vocation
There's hardly any room for such high sophistication
But go down to the Piper with a smile and open mind
'Cos good old-fashioned entertainment's what you'll always find.

Tracey Sharp

GRANDPA

I go to my grandpa's once every week,
And take him a meal or a pie,
I do him some shopping, he pays back the cash,
We talk of all under the sky.

We talk all about the football he loves,
With Sheffield Wednesday at home,
And gardens, and places, and countries and food,
TV and relatives who roam.

We talk of the past before I was born,
The way things worked when he was young,
How the new supertram is not like the old,
The old ways lost, to which he once clung.

I go home at three, Wednesday afternoon,
My weekly visit now complete,
To think when I'm back in mum's kitchen again,
Of next week's culinary treat.

Amanda L Wilson

COLOURS OF LOVE

I love you in all colours,
through red, black, pink and blue,
from harshest shades of misery,
to husky, dulcet hues.

I love you in all moods you have,
the feelings that tell all,
from rasping, raging anger,
to downy, willowy call.

I love you in all mediums,
in every shape and form,
and I'll love you 'til the sun goes down,
and rises in the dawn.

Caroline Phillips

TOUCHED BY LOVE

You came into my life
Teasing your way through my soul
Cutting like a knife - my heart
And then
You have taken on another role
Words spoken with such ease
I tried so hard to please
And now
We are to part

Our lives alone, will we regret
Or is it time we need
Separate ways to succeed
Our love postponed, alone
And then
Will you ever know
Just how much I loved you so

And will
You return to me, and both our lives fulfil
Will you
I am here waiting
As friend always, and lover too
Good luck my love in all you do
From my heart, forever true.

Rosemarie F Lockyer

THE TRAGEDY QUEEN

I've lived a whole lifetime under your gaze,
From a brief first appearance to starrier days.
Remember my youth when you saw me first,
Then how passing time has left me cursed.
Mine was the wedding which never took place,
The romances which left such a bitter taste.
Just listen to the wisdoms I have learned
Repeatedly getting my fingers burned.
And toughing it out across the years
You've seen my war paint run with tears.
Affairs and lovers by the dozen
Clasped to my magnificent bosom.
But when I enter the scene isn't it still
An almost palpitating thrill?
I capture your thoughts in a way that's unique
Half a nation listens when I speak.
Who knows which way my life will go?
Destiny lies in a weekly show.

Stephanie Francis

A GIRLS' NIGHT OUT

We tell our boyfriends we're having coffee,
But we're going out, my girlfriends and me,
Down to the nightclub, a girlies night out,
Up to the bar, hey it's my shout!
All settled down, drinks in hand,
Where's the stripper, where's the band?
The music starts, the lights grow dim,
On comes the stripper, then I realise it's him!
Up on stage for all to see,
I spy my boyfriend and he spots me.
I'm rigid with shock as I shed a tear,
He turns and says 'Didn't expect to see you here,
Don't be embarrassed, let's not have a row,
Stay and see the rest of the show.'
So for the rest of the night, rather than leave,
I watch my boyfriend do his striptease.
If we go out again, my girlfriends and me,
I think the next time we'll stick to coffee.

Zoe Woods

AEROBICS

Graceful as a butterfly
Creating perfect lines,
How I love to do aerobics
When I have some leisure time.

To have the perfect body
I strive and work so hard
Looking like some mystic goddess
In a bright green leotard.

I huff and puff and lunge and stretch
And never miss a beat.
I wonder if Jane Fonda
Has this problem with her feet?

I'm a lovely little mover
And I'm in the best of health.
Even when the pace gets faster
I can breathe all by myself!

I love it when the tutor
Says I move just like Wayne Sleep.
If I try next time I plié
I won't end up in a heap.

And yet I look no different
Despite every little ache.
Perhaps I'll drop my other hobby -
Eating sticky chocolate cakes!

Jane Elizabeth Drew

HAPPY TIMES

Sitting all alone at night,
    it seems to be my only right.
To rest from all the noise of day,
    I can at last steal faraway.

I curl up tight into a ball,
    and wait to hear the pleading call.
The one that says to me, *no sleep,*
    the one that rings my ears so deep.

A knock at the door disturbs my rest,
    at last arrives my crucial test.
Do I leave my comfy hub,
    and walk two miles to the pub?

Katie pleads, she's at my feet,
    'Think of all the men we'll meet.'
I think of all that surplus booze,
    and run in haste, to grab my shoes!

It's loud and noisy. Thumping head.
    Should I have stayed at home in bed?
Then, I see across the room,
    the man who makes my heart go *boom.*

But then I think, 'Well, why should I?'
    When all I ever do is try.
Instead I sit and chat to Kate,
    nothing beats a girl's best mate.

And if I'm feeling really low,
    I always know just where to go.
Any place, I just don't care,
    as long as my friend Kate is there.

A M Bolton

UNTITLED

A tear, a lake
A smile, the sun
Love on air to which we become one.
Needing, a yearning to which we succumb

Knowledge, friend or foe
depending on where we go
Life an ambition death a rest
before we go on to become our best.

Jackie Lines

PATCH

A shadow in the dark,
only a leaf,
moving through the night like a thief.
A noise over there,
just a mouse,
I'm still quite a bit from the house.
Footsteps on the ground,
I turn around,
all is quite,
not a sound.
Who is there? I shout,
silence is the only reply I get,
I begin to sweat.
My eyes move from side to side,
searching for a sign of life,
hoping that it hasn't a knife.
My heart is beating out of place,
hurry home is all I think,
and get myself something to drink.
The door is in sight,
where's the key,
O God, something touched my knee.
Running now with all my might,
I switch on the outside light.
I look around to meet my match,
but all that's there is
               my dog Patch.

Laura McCloskey

DON'T LOSE CONTROL

They met in the summer and then by the spring
We had total control of that naive young thing
Her devotion it grew but his love was untrue
Not a word did he say about love any day

Through glasses of rose she studied him
But she could not foresee the deception within
Clinging desperately for the love and the need
That she never received that never would be

The months turned to years and that's when the fears
Started floating around in her mind
But by this time the pride that she felt strong inside
Prevented her seeing his kind

She tried hard in vain to cover the pain
Of the love unreturned but the pain it still burned
The walls they closed in as she suffered this sin
Control had long left her sense was not in

There seemed only one choice piped up a small voice
But it wasn't the answer she knew deep inside her
Situations were desperate the battle begun
Naiveté lost intuition had won

And there up ahead was the light and the freedom
That she thought was long dead that she really was needing
Just courage that's all just a little at first
Testing the water she felt fit to burst

And then there she was
Her old self at last
And all of a sudden
The past became past . . .

Rebecca Pritchard

HOUSEBOAT

Your boat may be rocky on windy days
But you're free from the ties that blind and graze
Us ordinary mortals in our cosy abodes
Who pay the costs and sit on the roads.

Your boat may be damp in the fog
But no mortgage payments demand your endless slog
The boardwalk may shake come an earthquake
You will only roll but we'll certainly wake.

Your boat may be small in size
But what made you live so wise
The moon on the water, peewits on the wing
No wonder you always hear them sing.

Trudie Gordon

FORTY WINKS

He settles in the armchair
His fingers intertwined,
Eyes look a little dreamy
As if he's hypnotised.
'Not sleepy, only resting.'
At least, that's what he says,
His head is slowly drooping
Till chin on chest is laid.
Three hours or more recumbent
All tensions swept aside,
With face and form relaxing
On higher plains he flies.
As slowly, gently sliding
In soporific thrust,
Till cherub-like residing
In the arms of Morpheus.

On waking, yawns and stretches
In sedated tones he said,
'Not sleeping, only resting.
Feeling tired, I'm off to bed!'

Diane Lavery

TURN LOOSE THE DAYS

I was watching your train pulling away,
From the place that I live these days,
Thinking of how things used to be,
Back home with the boys and you and me,
Is it just me or are we growing apart?
You play the old tricks but I just can't laugh.
It seems to me we're not the same anymore.
So what did we make all those promises for?

I still think of the things we used to say,
About girls and money and getting away,
And all the old places we used to go,
And all the people we used to know.
Do all of these days have to be gone?
Couldn't I just carry them on?
But living in the past won't make things right
And living a lie won't help me sleep at night.

The hammer of days has taken its toll,
On the distant past that bound us all,
Red flames burn now blue and cold,
Turn loose the new days, turn out the old.
I feel the loosening of our ties of blood,
And the hand of time that split our pack,
I can't stop myself from walking away,
Turn loose the days, there's no holding them back.

David Collyer

LONELY

I once met a fella who I thought was the one
we parted company and he was gone
There were letters and calls the usual at first
but then someone else must have quenched his thirst
but still these feelings inside of me grew
I often thought if only he knew
I sat and wondered if we'd marry
because that would make me happy as Larry
So as you see I'm rather depressed
I think lonely is the word I'd rather suggest
I live in hope that one day yet
he'll come around so I can let
these feelings out, inside of me
and we can begin our life together ever happily
but that's the novel that never comes true
or is food for thought and something to chew
perhaps after all there is a cupid
to make all dreams come true!

Kate Bradley

BOKO

Hurt me, hate me,
See if I care.
As long as I love you,
I'll always be there.

Mock me, tease me,
It hurts me so deep.
But life goes on,
Even after I weep.

Touch me, kiss me,
I know it's your game.
Twist up my feelings,
And drive me insane.

Hit me, punch me,
with your nasty words.
Pretend I'm a fool,
One of the nerds.

Use me, abuse me,
Find someone new.
As long as I live,
I'll always love you.

Rebbecca Rampton (16)

UNTITLED

Have you ever had a boyfriend
   who meant the world to you.
A boyfriend you loved so very much,
   and miss him like I do,
Have you ever had a heartache,
   or felt such bitter pain.

Or shed your tears of sorrow,
   that fall like pouring rain.
If you've never known this feeling
   then I pray you never do.
For when God takes your boyfriend away,
   it breaks your world in two.

If I had a lifelong wish,
   it would not be wealth,
But just to have him back with me,
   in the very best of health.

Each time I see your photograph,
   you seem to smile and say,
Don't cry, I'm only sleeping,
   we'll meet again some day.

Lorna Hirst

STAYING ABREAST

The media relates to us
the hunger, thirst and shares
the realms of the unknown to us
and to anyone that cares

The media relates to us
a person with no name
a person with no home or clothes
but a person just the same

The media relates to us
an image just as seen
but we just turn the pages over
to us it's just a dream

The media relates to us
their sorrow, pain and fears
and empty eyes gaze in my soul
to fill my own with tears.

Zoe Simmons

BYE-BYE BABY

He captured my heart, then he changed my name,
Now he's left me alone, so my life's not the same.
In bed all I have to cuddle's my teddy,
But I'm no longer rushing to have his meal ready.
What once was a mess, I have cleaned of a man,
Now I read at the table, drinking beer from the can.
With just me it now matters what I think, how I feel,
And I'm starting to show what he made me conceal.
I'm no longer in shadows, don't change to fit in,
To be precious or sexy, I don't need to be thin.
So whenever I cry for our marriage on rocks,
I remind myself when I was washing his socks.
I thought if he left me, I'd not know what to do,
But I'm not only coping - I'm enjoying it too!

Sonia Phillips

A MOTHER'S CHILD

New-born babe, small and warm,
Safe, sheltered from all life's storm,
Soon he ventures on wobbly legs
Eager to seek adventures new,
Before you know, it's time for school

The years fly by
The child grows tall,
He sees the world through grown-up eyes,
Soon the child will be no more,
As now he opens life's next door,
for the sweet joys of youth, carefree laughter

The chance to find someone to share,
his hopes, his dreams, sometimes despair,
To kiss away his doubts, and fears,
To love him through the coming years,
But a mother's child he will always be,
When she first held him on her knee.

Mavis Henderson

UNTITLED

Once the candle stood alone
And filled the room with light,
Everything was shining,
It could even shine at night.

The brightness of the candle
Is fading very fast,
Darkness round the corner,
The blackness that'll last.

The candle that I watch
Is burning to its end,
The flame is my worst enemy,
The blackness, my best friend.

The yellow, like the sun,
Is turning into moon,
Slowly it clouds over,
And lightning strikes the room.

Now the candle's melting
Thunder steals its cry,
Its body burnt to ashes,
But still the flame survives.

The flame alone, grows smaller
No longer does it glow,
Darkness is surrounding,
No light will ever show.

Everything must change
For no longer is there light,
Without a candle, there's no flame,
Every day is night.

Simone Bertrand

TO DADDY

It's three in the morning
and I don't want to sleep
So Mummy and me
we lie there and speak

Mummy tells me stories
that are all about you
But don't worry, I know
they can't all be true

She told me how you both met
and how I came to be
That you shouldn't have but if you hadn't
I would never be me

Mummy said Daddy
was sometimes bad
And how many times
you made her sad

But through it all
she always loved you
And I want you to know
now I love you too

Despite all this
I know you're not really a *baddie*
and I just want to say
I'm so glad you're my
Daddy.

A Hyndman

FIT FOR WHAT

I'm really into keeping fit
I work out everyday
To get my body nice and trim
And hear all my friends say

My God you're looking healthy
My God you're looking good
I wish that I could look like you
I would do if I could

But just stop there, it's all a trap
It's not worth all the strain
You sweat and grunt, bend and stretch
All in the fitness name

It's cannot eat this, must not do that
It's counting calories
It's getting up at crack of dawn
With chapped and aching knees

It's track suit on then off you go
Jogging day and night
Fifteen times around the park
Avoiding dogs that bite

Dodging cars and cyclists
And every jogger's dread
With eyes fixed firmly on the ground
To watch just where you tread.

So before you take up jogging or even something worse
Stop a while and think, take note of my last verse

I look aloft and question . . .?
I really must ask why . . .?
Has all this got but just one aim
To be fit when I die . . . !

Ian C Dayer

THANK YOU TO REG

Reg, I know that you
make people mad,
but you are the best
The Street has had.
You make me laugh
after a busy day,
wish you could swagger
down our way.
Your saucy smile
brightens up the screen,
and your debonair walk
is quite a dream.
If I should ever see
you in passing,
please give me a *twiddle*
with your glasses.
Handsome and charming
you will always be,
if ever in Devon
please come to tea.

Neta Holmes

UNTITLED

It's Monday, the time, ten past five,
For my favourite seat I dive.
I take the phone off the hook so it cannot ring,
Because *Home and Away* is about to begin.
A soon as it's finished the channel is changed,
For a soap, I reckon, is top of the range.
It has to be *Neighbours* I hear you say,
And you'd be right, as sure as day is day.
But for excitement, *EastEnders* is the one,
Even though Den and Angie have long since gone.
Both Sharon and Grant have had a lot to face,
Running the Queen Vic in their place.
One thing's for sure, I'm always there,
To watch the residents of Albert Square.
And after all this, I still need more,
So it's time to turn to Channel 4..
It's *Brookside* which I watch with pleasure,
But there's one more soap I can't begin to measure.
It's a soap that no other soap could beat,
That's my visit down Coronation Street.
There's always something new to learn,
In Bet's friendly pub *The Rovers Return*.

C Rawlinson

RHAPSODY TO THE MEMORY OF B BAKER
'Once in the halls she walked and she was war,
angel of war, angel of agony, lighting men to death.'
Aeschylus

Bev Baker! Weaned on viper's venom - *Beast*
   In phantom human form, crossbred with crows'
Cunning, coal-eyes to warm a carrion feast
   And kindle pleasures as a life's blood flows;
Like Furies wreaking wrath on erring man,
   You spiked your system with the heights of pain:
Inspired by anguish, mortal minds may span
   The hidden cosmos, ecstasy to gain!

Gore-lust rising in a wave of passion,
   On your shoulders murders piling steeply;
Still you hungered for an extra ration,
   One ambition stirring cold and deeply:
You sought your heaven, stunned your anxious heart;
Embraced full death, and fled your living part.

Simon Hall

EASTENDERS

'Twas a nice morning
Stall holders were calling
To punters who were strolling
To find the best bargain
I trust you're aware
That this is *Albert Square*
Where unkindness is rare
'Cos we're people who care
We've a nice *rub a dub*
A cafe wiv good grub
A mechanic to fix yer
Jam jar from the dealer
But for a chat and a rumour
Wiv a touch of good humour
Then make way my pet
To the market launderette
If it's fruit that you want
A dress for the restaurant
Then don't push or panic
Our spots outside the Vic
If you walk down Bridge Street
And find all is not neat
We do have a keeper
Who's a green-fingered sweeper
So turn your mince pies
To your TV agendas
Is it films for the night
Or just good old *Eastenders*.

S Mc Gill

BOBBY'S GONE AWAY

Little Bobby so sweet and caring
Not like others who want to do sharing
Husbands or lovers.
Working the oven at the diner.
Soon that will be behind her
Sometimes sad especially when Sam is
Bad, but usually happy and glad.
Small and petite. Neat and quick on her
Feet to help.
A little treasure as Pippa and Ailsa
Would say, yes, the best in Summer Bay.
As the surf rolls over and waves break
Against the shore,
She's gone from the scene, seen no more.
Like hands waving, the waves of the bay
Seem to say goodbye Bobby.

Janette Turner

DEAR PERCY

The soap character I most like on TV,
Has to be dear grumpy old Percy,
He does not suffer fools at all,
Under his glare the toughest fall,
Time and again he hates what's said,
If looks could kill they'd drop down dead.

Coronation Street is where he lives,
Much free advice he always gives,
Everyone tries to avoid the man,
They dodge him if ever they can,
Percy knows just what they are doing,
One can always see new trouble brewing.

Despite his many faults on the table,
He will always help others when he's able,
For him modern life is far too fast,
Percy would prefer the long gone past,
In those days he fought for peace and freedom,
He's beginning to feel there was no reason.

Today the crime wave is very bad,
Percy hates it and can only get mad,
In his young days it would not be,
Children were punished over Father's knee,
If only discipline was back once more,
Perhaps this character would not feel sore.

Nicola Scott

A SOAP FAN

I love every minute,
I wish I were in it.
    A soap.

I'm happy, I'm glad,
I feel good, I feel sad,
    That's soap.

The Street, The Farm
Don't mean any harm.
    It's soap.

Home and Away,
Neighbours here to stay,
    More soap.

I can't get enough
Smooth or rough,
    Any soap.

In the past I was loopy
The sixties a groupie
    But soap
Has made me so dopey
I'm now an old soapie!

Hurrah for soap.

Chris Maddison

EASTENDERS - ALBERT SQUARE

The Old Vic is the *hub* of place,
    Where all the square can come
Sad and bad, good and glad
    'Tis here the punters run.

There's Pauline there and Arthur too
    Amonst the motley crowd
Ricky whining, Sharon shining
    And Nigel shouting loud.

Michelle, and Pat our suffering Mum
    Phil, the wicked lad
Mark, Kathy, Cindy too
    Not forgetting Grant the cad.

Trickie Dickie he's no fool
    With his wily charm
Ian Beale's a scheming chap
    One day he'll come to harm.

Wimpish Sam's a silly boy
    By pals so easily led
Perhaps one day he'll get it right
    And settle down instead.

Arson, fraud, the car lot's had
    Its share of ups and downs.
Our Frank - why he, of course,
    Is just the king of clowns.

Vicky, Martin, one day will be
    The top ones in the square
With Ian's twins and Janine too
    The future's starting here.
Albert Square is full of life, normal everyday -
    Winners, losers, all; The Square is here to stay.

Mollie D Earl

BROOKSIDE

Liverpudlian accents and drama
Murders, affairs and religion
Has Brookside just got a bad karma?
Who cares, it's only television.
Isn't it?

Margaret and Beth are young lovers
Now confused about life's complexity
About their love lives with each other
Or does it come down to sexuality.
Doesn't everything?

Now Jimmy, the man of the moment
The junkie, rescued by Ron
Is in an acute state of torment
Thanks to drugs and killing Ron's son.
Do we care?

Didi and Bev are Ron's women
Contrasting though it can be seen
One has spent her life with religion
The other wants to be karaoke queen.
What for?

Will Sinbad and Mandy get together?
With her husband interred out the back
Will they learn to live with each other?
Without feeling they've gone through the rack.
Why shouldn't they?

Where does the material come from?
All of this trouble and strife
Sadness, corruption, deception
We're told that soaps simulate life.
Is it reality?

Kirsteen Sinclair

DEN AND ANGIE WATTS - EASTENDERS

He kept on breaking her heart of gold
And the marriage seemed to be getting cold
Minutes, hours through the day and night
Were hard to pass without a fight
The feelings forever getting colder
The rows forever getting bolder
A frantic search for something civil to say
As the stony silence ran into a day
But they kept up the fiction of a happier life
The pretence they were a loyal husband and wife
The affairs, the rows, the hatred, the lies
The bust-ups, reconciliation's, and poignant good-byes
The smallest thing could cause a rift
And their marriage vows went far adrift
At the end of the day, shattered dreams
And the marriage splitting at the seams
The whole time a mixture of love and hate
Passion and poison from the very first date
Then they looked back with obvious regret
At some times to cherish and some to forget
His work and her drinking hid each broken heart
When they faced up to life, living apart.

Stephanie Davies (15)

BROOKSIDE

Brookside Close is a scally's haven,
The wheeling and dealing and close shaving
Barry Grant, what a scouse,
Whilst Mandy Jordasche is quiet as a mouse,
There's Jimmy Corkhill, what a mess,
There's even a Mo! Or is it *two ton tess*
Margaret and Beth, now there's a pair,
Rather strange, even odd, a little bit queer
What about Sinbad, full of life,
I wish the scriptwriters, would find him a wife.
Look at Ron, the mid-life-crisis-man,
If any one can tame him, I'm sure Bev can,
Dee-Dee his ex, has lost faith in the church,
Whereas Derek, her brother, left
Mags in the lurch.
Now a new family, a son in the army,
There's secrecy amongst them,
Else it's me going barmy.
Did you see it last week, the lingerie party?
The items were tacky, rather tarty,
Patricia Farnham, Marie-Ann too,
Didn't know, just what to do,
Their faces were crimson, their
Looks said it all,
But the rest of the girls were
Having a ball.

Bobby MacDuff

SOAP ADDICT?

I plan my tea around Brookside
Neighbours is lunchtime break.
Home and Away every day
Emmerdale Thursdays make.

I live and learn with Young Doctors
And Coro' is right up my street.
I visit the East end twice a week
The Ewings I'd love to meet.

I'm locked up in H Block quite often
And always get caught by The Bill.
I guess I'm just hooked by the soaps
Can't help it! I think that they're brill!

Rachel Robinson

THE PUB TO THE SHED

Anyone can fall in love in Albert Square
There's a pub and cafe and a laundrette there
If you go in the Vic, that's the pub in the square
Watch out for Grant Mitchell, he's the landlord there.
Sharon, Grant's wife is sort of nice.
She's been with Phil, Grant's brother once or twice.
Phil has a lock up in the square
There's a few dodgy deals talked about there
Phil loves Kathy, she's a Beale, she was married to Pete
He was killed! Trod on the wrong feet
Kathy's son Ian is a bit of a swine I wouldn't want
Him as a son of mine.
Ian grabbed Pete's stall as soon as he died
Sold it to Mark he's very ill
He's still in love with his ex wife, Jill.

Pauline and Arthur Fowler live in the square
They're Mark's parents, an outspoken pair.
Arthur has an allotment on the square
In his shed on that allotment there, Arthur Fowler
Had an illicit affair, there he wooed Mrs Hewitt
Arthur, oh Arthur, how could you do it.
Pauline, Arthur's wife she found out and promptly kicked him out.
She didn't half shout at Mrs Hewitt who still
Loved Arthur and he knew it.

Frank and Pat Butcher do a bit of this and a bit of that
Frank's car lot went up in smoke, now him and Pat
Are well and truly broke
Pat had a drink and decided to drive
Finished up doing six months inside.

Jean Spearing

UNTITLED

I'll sit down get comfortable and turn you on
If I can find the remote control, just where has it gone
Here it is phew that was close
The thought of missing you is gross
Lauren or Beth, Brad which is it to be
Gaby and Wayne are arguing again I see
Poor Stephen and Phoebe what a shame
You were a lot happier until Russell came
And with daughter baby Hope
It all happens on my number one soap
Helen I think you're a brick
And what's happening with Debbie and Rick

Twenty minutes goes too soon
Now they're playing the *Neighbours* tune.
It is such a great sorrow
Having to wait until tomorrow
Another twenty four hours is how long I'll have to wait
But I've got it on tape so I can watch it till late.

Debbie Dulieu

WAR OF THE SOAPS

Emmerdale and Coronation Street are with channel three,
Whilst Eastenders are on channel one BBC.
Brookside on its own belongs to Channel Four
Channel two don't have a soap, oh what a bore,
The Beeb are trying to win viewers from channel three,
Not satisfied with that they have upset Brookside for me,
What a childish lot of spoil sports the programme planners must be,
They are mucking up my favourite soaps, on my TV.
Which one will I watch, I must use my common sense,
I really like to watch them all it makes me so tense,
Ah just a moment whilst I think,
Before this confusion drives me to drink.
The *Beeb* give me a half hour show,
Adverts on the others shortens the flow.
This dilemma has me puzzled, I really don't know,
Perhaps I'll have to save up, and buy a *video*.
Gosh an idea has struck me, to save a lot of fuss,
Why not stay in at weekends and watch the *omnibus*.

R Butler

NEIGHBOURS

Every week-day, just after one
    I catch up on the Ramsay fun
There is intrigue and romance too
    They really are right on cue
There is sea, surf and sunshine
    With a galaxy of stars
I can almost feel the sunshine
    And ride in Lou's old cars

Hotels, coffee bars and swimming pools
    Seem to set the scene
Even work seems glamorous, this side of the screen

Brad should stick to surf boards
    And leave the girls to Shane
He goes 'round breaking hearts, it really is a shame

There is one thing for certain
    That if you visit there
You will find the warmest welcome
    And sample Aussie beer!

Irene Clegg

BROOKSIDE

Poor Jimmy is a druggie, Tony Dixon's dead.
Margaret has got problems with lovers Carl and Beth.
Mandy is sick with worry, she buried Trevor deep
But Sinbad's shoulder is handy on which for her to weep.

Our Ron is quite exhausted with Beverley and the babe,
The sleepless nights are killing for a fellow of his age.
D-D's all forgiving, she's really quite a saint,
And Simon is oh so creepy with his bible punching mates.

Poor Katie has been stupid, she's fallen for his line,
Her frowns are getting deeper and more worried all the time.
There's Mick busy making pizzas that never seem to sell,
They don't make any money, but manage very well.

Such a lot of drama on this most famous Close,
Channel Four and Brookside
The soap I love the most.

Dorothy M Arrowsmith

THE STREET

It's almost seven thirty, I must get to my seat.
Everything comes to a halt for Coronation Street.

Can't wait to see what happens when Dessy gets found out,
Odds on he'll be the loser - the double crossing lout.

And what about poor Derek? This time he's gone too far.
He's just spent all their savings on a clapped out motorcar.

My favourite is Ken Barlow, will he let down his hair?
And allow Denise to trim it with tender loving care.

As for Percy Sugden, he's facing trying times.
Instead of saintly Emily, he's landed crosshatch Grimes.

I'm glad to see that buxom Bet has found a man at last.
He's bound to drive her crazy, 'cos he's very very fast!

It looks as though Mike Baldwin is down to his last pound.
But good old faithful Alma will always be around.

Since Alf's old mini market has had a change of staff,
We can count on Reg and Maureen to give us all a laugh.

I really wish poor Curly could find himself a mate.
If he doesn't get a move on he'll be past his sell by date.

Don and Ivy Brennan have had their share of grief.
Perhaps they'll have a pools win and retire to Tenerife.

Gail and Martin and their kids - their lives seem full of joy.
Perhaps there's something to be said for having a toy boy!

Now Jack and Vera Duckworth have had their ups and downs,
But still they keep on smiling - just like the circus clowns.

Not forgetting the McDonalds - we all know the score.
Anyone who looks at Liz will end up on the floor!

Kevin, Sally, Rosie too, they almost lost their way,
But Rita's little legacy has gone and saved the day.

There's Tanya, Betty, Racquel too (she really is a treat).
But then everybody is first class in Coronation Street.

E Wilson

POEM ON SOAPS

When I moved to Dallas, it was with the understanding
It would be away to a place which was known as Knots Landing.
I got in with my Neighbours but life was incomplete,
Until I met the simple folk down Coronation Street.
When I ran short of cash I went to the money lenders
I soon found help round Albert Square in London's great *Eastenders*.
When I thought it was time, I went north by British Rail,
It was only two days later when I arrived at Emmerdale.
I joined a Country Practice as I needed The Young Doctors guide.
With all my aches and pains I hitched along to Brookside.
I decided to Take The High Road, I certainly didn't dally,
As before too long I was visiting friends *the people of the valley*.
After taking in the scenery, I surely had my fill,
I came to a Crossroads in my life, I had a run in with The Bill.
It was time to get a move on, I travelled night and day
Thinking about the friends I'd made both at Home and Away.
I started feeling weary, I knew it was time to rest.
So I asked the Flying Doctors to take me to Falcon Crest.
A brief encounter with Angela Channing, told me it was time to go!
I packed my bags and fled to the sun, settling down in Eldorado.

Kay M Reid

CORONATION SOAP

I always like watching the street
With Bet and staff at Rovers, giving residence a treat.
Rita's so prim and proper.
Jack's always coming a cropper -
With his wife Vera Duckworth - always having so much to say
Oh Sally and Kevin, have another baby on the way
Mavis' Derek Wilton's such a drip
Missed the coach on a day trip
I ask you - who'd be such a fool - losing his job at school
There is Des Barnes who works at the bookie
Now is it Racquel or Tanya his bit of nookie
Reg and Maureen finally got married, that's hard to swallow,
Now blow me Percy and Maude are set to follow
Alf and Audrey sold the corner shop
If only the knew retirement would be such a flop.
Ken and Denise are making friends
Curly and staff at Betterbuys are trying new trends
Why not ring Ivy and Don for a taxi
Next time you're on a spree
And visit the cafe with Alma, Gale, Mike and Philis for tea.

D Ayshford

THE TV SOAPS

Soaps! Soaps! Now let me see!
Which has the most attraction for me?
There's *Emmerdale Farm,* with its country charm,
Though life in the village is not so calm!

Next comes Eastenders,
My goal is the *Vic*, its warmth and bartenders
A cockney myself, I quite like the *lingo*
Heard in my childhood, long long ago!

Then there is Brookside!
In their neat little houses, problems divide them,
There's weddings and birthdays, laughter and hate,
We witness it all and follow their fate!

What makes me, I wonder,
Want to see *Neighbours*, down under!
But I check the time and pull up my chair,
Let no one disturb me! Callers beware!

But not least, is Coronation Street!
The soap of all soaps, the hardest to beat!
We meet each week at the Rovers Return,
To know more about them, that's where we learn!

Now what else can I say?
But trust the soaps have come to stay!
I enjoy them all in various degree
But *Coronation Street* is the one for me!

Nancy Smith

CARLY PARKER'S VIEW TOWARDS TV SOAPS

My favourite soap is Neighbours
But Eastenders is good as well,
Especially since Shelly
Has moved in with Michelle.
I like The Bill and Coronation Street,
But Home and Away's a bore.
Country Practice and Flying Doctors
Are also very poor.
I like excitement and adventure,
I don't like things to drag.
That's why I enjoy The Bill,
That's why Flying Doctors is a dag!
Now in Neighbours I like Brad,
Boy! is he hunky.
But I don't like Lou or Philip,
They are *way* too chunky.
In Eastenders I like Frank,
He can be very funny.
But I do feel sorry for him really,
'Cos he's having problems with his money.
Now you know what I watch on telly,
While eating chocolate and strawberry jelly.
I *am* a soap addict as you can see,
I wonder if *I'm* your winner to be!

Carly Parker

THE STREET

What would we do without life in the *Street*
Somehow our lives would seem incomplete
We've come to know the characters as if they were friends of ours.
The staff of The Rovers who serve behind the bars!
Bette, Bet, Tanya, Racquel and Jack
Complement each other, 'cause Alec won't be back.
Reg has married Maureen and they've brought the corner shop
And Maud has trapped poor Percy and caught him on the hop!
Ken has finished with Deirdre, Denise is his new attraction
She's trying to play it cool in response to Ken's reaction!
Curly has his moments, but Des is unlucky in love
And now, because he's *played away* he's had to make a move.
Derek with his pipe dreams, Mavis with her moans
Work hard at doing everything to keep up with *the Jones*
Now Alf and Audrey have retired and he's elected Mayor
Audrey's off on shopping sprees buying all new clothes to wear.
Mike and Alma love and hate and often disagree
I suppose they'll get their act together e-ven-tu-ally
Kevin and Sal, Martin and Gail, Ivy, Don and more
Liz and Jim and the twins and those who live next door
Rita in *The Kabin* does many a kindly deed
Help and advice she offers to those who are in need
Bernards proposed to Emily, now these two will be one
Vera's complaining and Terry's on the run!
Now we must make a trip and travel far down *memory-lane*
And think of Violet, Minnie and Martha, Hilda and her Stan
Old Uncle Albert, Alan, Elsie, Annie and Jack
Ernie Bishop and Mr Swindly, never will be back.
There are also many others who would make this tale complete
So God bless all the actors who play characters in
                                                    The Street.

Jean Buckmaster

SOAPS

I have a yen for *Dirty Den*,
With Angie in the *Vic*,
And all the hopes and fears in soaps,
Down the years which pass so quick.

It's true the *Street* has been a treat
With tenants old and new,
And all the *Rovers* customers
Return to taste the brew.

In Emmerdale, when it blows a gale,
To the *Woolpack* they all flock,
The lambs which gambol in the fields
Quite recently had a shock.

Down under, Adam makes blunder after blunder,
Both *Home and Away*,
However, it would surely seem,
That this soap has come to stay.

Everybody is friendly in *Neighbours*,
They flit in and out and round about,
Full of goodwill, doing each other favours,
True *Aussies* all, OK it's my *shout*.

In *Brookside,* life's no easy ride,
Life has its ups and downs,
Muggings and crime, but they still have their pride,
There's smiles amongst all the frowns.

So we'll say farewell for now,
And think of the pleasure we've had,
The good times and bad, happy and sad.
Odd times we've said I really must vow,
I won't switch on again but it would cause me pain,
So here's to the next soap and fond memories remain.

A G Holmes

SOAP FOLK

My absolutely favourite soap
Is the one called . . . er . . whatsit street.
It's about the ordinary friendly folk
That we all just love to meet.

There's Tracey Barlow, just left school.
(Ken and Deirdre's darling daughter).
She has a way with older folk;
If they're upset, she'll make them fraughter.

Then poor old Phylis has one desire -
To give her heart to Percy.
How will she cope when it's revealed
That Maude has done the dirty?

Both Mave and Derrick soldier on,
He just wants to earn a living.
So half their savings he invests,
To be employed - Mave is *so* forgiving.

Racquel is such a lovely girl
Her faith in Des is true and sweet
She trusts her fiends both old and new
But wait till she finds there's a cheat in the street!

Gayle and Martin do so well
Despite friction with the in-laws.
But there's trouble brewing I'm afraid
From that staff nurse - you know - *droopy drawers*.

Sally and Kev are a real good couple
Though he's a first class pig-head.
And Curly wants to watch his step
Or I fear he'll end up dead.

Whilst Bet and the rest carry on with their life,
There'll always be intrigue, trouble and strife.

Augusta Waite

THESE THREE SOAPS ARE FOR ME

Every day I sit in front of the telly,
Sometimes so much I forget to take off one wellie.
Neighbours I watch the most,
Sitting down with my piece of toast.
The scenery is absolutely brill,
The birds they sing a lot I'm sure they must eat trill.
I like Brad and Wayne the best,
Because to they are they are better than the rest.
But they are all really very good.

At night time I watch Coronation Street,
And to me this is really a great treat.
I put some wood on the fire so as to turn up the heat,
Then I sit down and put my slippers on my feet.
Percy and Maude are good for each other,
And I think Racquel should become a mother.
Curly please stay as you are,
And then I can admire you from afar.
Your cheeky grin, and the glasses you wear,
Make you look quite sexy, but please do something about your hair.

And last but not least,
I'm down to Eastenders.
Tricky Dicky and good old Ricky too,
But how I do miss lovely Lou.
There's the Beales, Fowlers, and Butchers there,
Grant and Phil aren't they a pair.
My poem is now at an end I have done my good deed,
Now it has finished you can all have a good read.
I hope you enjoy this as I'm not very good,
My mum sometimes says to me your as short and thick as two
                                         planks off wood.

A Ashley

UNTITLED

The amazing thing about soaps
Is that you never have time to mope.
From Ramsay Street to Coronation Street
There's honestly no retreat.

They make you laugh, they make you cry
Someone gets married unfortunately they die.
Fashion trends are usually way out
But I'm sure they'll catch up I have no doubt.

Why there's Phoebe, Annalise and Beth
Not forgetting Jack, Annie Sugden and dear Seth.
Poor old Mavis, Rita and Bet
And lots of others we haven't yet met.

We travel world wide each day
Watching, listening to all they say.
The plots they sometimes leave us guessing
I'll keep watching there'll be no messing.

We'll never know what keeps us watching
These people we treat like an immortal being.
But it's nearly part of our history
And will I'm sure remain a complete mystery.

G Pughsley

ALL MY SOAPS

The day for me starts with a smile
I think I will watch TV for a while
First I watch Families, oh whatever next
As I hunt round for the teletext
Next the phone rings, my friends tonight
Want to meet
I can't possibly go.
I'll miss Coronation Street
And what about Brookside, the
Stories are endless
And let's not forget the brilliant
Eastenders.
I tell them I'm ill, I caught flu yesterday
Well I can't tell the truth, I
Daren't miss Home and Away
The day ahead stretches, so much
Viewing to do
I've got Neighbours, Country
Practice and Young Doctors too
I have my tea and take a rest
What's on now, Take the High Road
Next
I have my bath and out comes the ale
Just in time to watch Emmerdale
It's getting late now as I look
At the clock
Last soap for today
Is the superb Cell Block.

Pam Harrison

MY NORMAL DAY

What a hectic day in the office, I fancy a beer
Anyone going out? Not even a leer
I went home to my bedsit poured myself a G & T
Ate my TV dinner sat upon my knee
Knock, knock, knock went my door
Ring, ring, ring went my bell.
It was the girls from work, 'Let's go out what the hell.'
I slipped into my new dress, russled with my hair
Rushed down to the local, the men are tasty there
After Vodka number two and G & T number four
I felt so alive, I wanted some more
We danced on the tables and smooched with all the men
I'm counting the hours for the party again.

Lynn McAuley

THE MARKSMAN

With sprightly step the marksman treads the bracken path
And scans the heavens above with practised eye,
Lifting the rifle to his shoulder, takes steady aim and fires,
Blasting the living creature from his playground in the sky.

His hound, with snuffling nose, runs forward through the gorse
To forage for the fallen body, discovers where it lay,
And in his soft jaws retrieves the limp and feathered corpse
Which moments since soared freely through the sunlit day.

Added to the brace, it's numbered now with them,
Tied by foot, eyes dulled, with broken wing,
Once it tossed on currents' flow and roamed the distant wastes;
How could they kill the dignity of such a splendid thing?

Ann Rutherford

THE BUSKER

Sad and lonely,
the busker in his corner.
Shunned by the masses,
acknowledged by few.
His blue face,
tired and weary.
Frail hands hold his mouth organ
to chapped lips.
A broken tune
rings through the alley,
echoing to the streets beyond.

No-one listening,
ashamed at the clutter.
Pennies drop as duty,
when they scurry past.
Memories of how it used to be
mean nothing to him.
Crumpled and worn,
huddled in a doorway
good days pass, like bad.

Tracey Ross

FATE

Living someone else's life,
reciting other peoples lines,
with my life designed,
will I ever find the real me?
The only words I ever spoke
are written down in prose or verse.
Just a passage to view the real me
I have not the power to voice my thoughts,
confidence will never stray.
Living beneath the sheets
will I ever reach the final word,
will I ever speak a word of me?

David Quick

LONELY FRIENDS

Peewits cried on startled wings
flying up from new ploughed land,
for winter was but a frost away
leading autumn by the hand.
A lowering skyline closed in on the horizon
light losing its battle to the falling dusk,
wings whistled high overhead
the sound of unseen flighting ducks.
Whistling widgeon and peewits cry
both lonely friends in a fading sky,
stark landscape kissed by a freezing mist
as we head home my dog and I.

Roger Stokes

MOTHER

A mother is an angel
who's always there for you
she wipes away your tear drops
whenever you feel blue.
She's always there to lend a hand
a smile upon her face
she really is your best friend
in this the human race.
Oh when you are a baby, she holds you in her arms
and then as you grow older, she spoils you
with her charms.
At night when you go sleeping, she tucks you up in bed
and when you are a sickly thing
she cradles your head.
Oh how I love my mother, for being there for me
Dear mum you are the greatest gift
that God could give to me.

C Bampton

SPARE TIME

Spare time is something we like,
To do whatever we please,
Some like to rest and let it
Slip on by,
Others like to dance and have
a good time,
There's so much you can do.
Just try anything,
Maybe taking a walk, I find it's
good to talk.
Maybe someone is lonely and
in need of your time.
it's all your own, there's no
need to rush.
It's lovely when we have a lot
We should be thankful for
what we've got.

Susan O'Shea

WHO KNOWS

Clouds closing in all around,
Sky all black,
Sea all green,
People all around,
Rushing to where?
Don't want to talk,
Just turn and go the other way.

Does anyone know
What's going on?
Then tell me then perhaps I'll understand.

Shutting off,
Don't want to know,
Ready to run,
To get away,
But where would I run?
God knows where,
It looks so easy,
To turn and run.

The road looks inviting,
Perhaps I'll go,
But I'll leave behind
All that matters
But who cares?

I stand all alone
People don't want to know,
My head keeps spinning
It's so easy to go.

Perhaps i'll go along that road
Who knows?
Perhaps I'll just stop the world
And get off
Perhaps! Who knows?

Roseann Standring

IT ALL STARTS HERE

Saturday night and it all starts here,
I'll just pop out for one quick beer.
One turns to two and reaches eight,
Next time I count I've drunk a crate.

To the *Frisco Disco* we go for a bop,
My friends and I could shimmy till we drop.
Any nice lookers, I can see none at all,
In fact it should be called the Ugly Bug Ball.

Dancing to *Kylie* and doing the Loco
'Seen anyone nice' - I should cocoa!
That one there keeps giving me the eye,
Why do I always get the nerds I sigh.

Mellow songs resound and my suitor draws near,
He desires a slowie, it's really quite clear.
Our bodies sway and he wants to see me more,
As soon as the lights go up I'm out the door.

At the end of the night, time for a kebab,
Eat it down quickly and jump in a cab.
All back to my place, me and the crew,
Coffee and chats and fights for the loo.

Sunday morning and it all stops here,
My head is throbbing after that quick beer.
Day turns to night, I wish my head to mend,
Never again
At least not until next weekend!

Lisa Wakeham

DEEP IN MY SOUL

Deep in my soul,
Lies a complication that expands,
Beyond understanding,
Of the one who held my hand.

Tears and tension,
Frustration and fear,
A cry for help,
That no-one wishes to hear.

No-one sharing a part of me,
No-one to see my misery,
One day pain will rest behind,
That day I long to find.

Rachel Imm

WHEN LOVERS SLEEP

So pure can be illicit love
Unsoiled, when lovers sleep,
Imbued with sacred reverie
Awake, they cease to keep.

Like children in their chaste embrace
Devoid of sin, all guile.
The sole abidance of their lust
Resides within a smile.

All fears that stir the soul within,
Bow down, retiring deep.
Contentment sings the lullaby
Of life . . . when lovers sleep.

Mandy Chambers

COUNTRY LOVERS

Do you remember when we were young?
The world seemed a safer place.
We'd cycle in groups from our old country town
And explore village lanes and 'green' space.

No fear of anything entered our heads,
Just, 'What'll we do today?'
Our gang had such fun and lots of good games
To play, 'mid the fields of hay.

As soon as the Spring has warmed the cold air
We'd want to be let 'out to play'
Exploring the lanes and streams all around,
Observing new things every day.

From bird's nest to frog's spawn
And naming the plants that we saw in the hedgerows so green.
Hear the Cuckoo . . . and the Skylark . . . and all of the birds,
We would make lists of the things that we'd seen.

Then all through the Summer we'd be out in the sun,
The days seemed so endless and warm.
The colours and scents of the flowers around,
We even saw bees in a swarm!

Autumn was marked by the colour of leaves
Before they began to fall down.
We had bonfires too that left lazy smoke plumes . . .
You can't do that living in town!

Then Winter brought us some more things to do,
As wrapped up so warm, we would go
To gather up nuts and wood for the fires
And come home with a good, healthy glow!

Jennifer Jenkins

THE GERANIUM

Bold as brass, bright as paint,
A strumpet flower, that's what you are!
A blushing, self-confessed thing
With raddled cheeks and wanton flaunt.
No art, no play of love, no subtitles are yours
You state your price and give your worth
And to the highest bidder bow.
And yet still my scarlet-dazzled eyes
Must grant you grudging place
For when winter comes, and age and dark
There's only you to give me hope.

B Pritchard

CHOSEN

Chosen in
the morning sun
the elder currants
gleam;
a starling
hops careless
on the branch.
In unconscious rivalry
he flies
hurriedly away.

Driekje de Boer

FOREVER IN YOUR HEART

The autumn days grow short and cold
The winter is soon here
But you bring spring into my life
Wherever you are near.

The months go by, long and hard
Whenever we're apart
Please promise me, I will stay
Forever in your heart.

David McMahon

COUNTRY CAMEOS

I see the horses nod their heads as up the field they go
With steady plod of heavy hooves, their progress sure and slow;
The ploughshares cutting through the earth; the ploughman's
                                        steadfast stride;
While flocks of seagulls, gleaming white, down to the furrows
                                        glide:
This pleasant sight of yesteryear I never thought could be
In years to come, the substance of a treasured memory.

I smell the scent of new-mown hay beneath the summer skies
And skimming low, above the swathes, the nesting swallow flies;
The hay-wains come and toiling men to gather in the hay;
And hedgerows snatch the straying strands the breeze has blown
                                        their way;
Then ricks are built beside the gate that leads into the lane:
These sunny scenes of memory's eye, how they come back again!

The pleasing rows of barley stooks, alas, are seen no more
In mellow golden harvest fields, as in the days of yore.
The setting sun no more will cast long shadows from the sheaves -
No haven for the harvest mouse or for the nest it weaves.
Yes, they are gone, the old things. Everything is new.
It's the cheaper and the quicker ways that will only do!
Yet though the years have brought such change, bright cameos I
                                        see -
The pictures painted in my mind Time cannot take from me!

Margaret Barns

PRICELESS

I strolled the lane the other day
And saw the jewels by the way -
Wild flowers shining in the sun;
Some bluebells, cowslips - every one
A masterpiece, a pure creation:
Delighting in each situation.

I heard the birds both far and near -
A wren brought music to my ear;
A robin, blackbird, thrush, and then
A cuckoo piped its song for ten.
I watched the swallows twist and dart.
I found a nest - a work of art.

Scent from the hawthorn hedge in flower
Was pungent at that early hour.
A butterfly flipped past; I caught
A glimpse of yellow as it sought
A place to rest its beating wings.
There skulked a beetle, one that stings.

The trees looked fresh in crisp spring-green,
As though the winter had not been.
A stoat ran out, and then a vole.
A muddy heap . . . sign of a mole.
So much to see, to smell, revere,
I wished the lane went on for e'er.

The sun went in, the rain came down
Yet still the jewels twinkled on,
They sparkled more, their colours glowed
Enlivening the old, grey road.
I spent three hours of total glee
And all I'd seen, heard, smelt was *free!*

J Maitland

THE SUMMER HAS COME

The grass is green,
The horse eats hay.
The blossom trees blossom.
The rose gets redder.
The flower gets prettier.
The sunflower gets taller.
The summer is here,
It's time to celebrate
All through the year!

Stefanie Thomas

UNTITLED

Let's talk about something that's never seen
Let's talk about something that has no mean,
Let's talk about something that's not usually said,
Let's talk about something which hasn't been written so not yet read,
Let's talk about something that's never existed,
Let's talk about something really sick and twisted,
Let's talk about something raw and sordid,
Let's talk about something cold, dead and morbid,
Let's talk about something corroded and has stink to high heaven,
Or let's not talk at all, let's think.
Let's think about what's left behind, inside and around the mind,
How much longer to catch up with wasted time
What we already know and what's left to find,
Let's think about seclusion and destitution,
Let's think deep down amongst all the confusion,
Let's think about poison and pornography,
Let's not think about English and geography,
Let's think about mental suffering misery and torment,
There's nothing wrong in being despondent,
Or let's not think at all, let's be,
Let's be dangerously perverse, overpowering with
                                      unhealthy abnormality.
Let's be incredibly faithful and full of Christianity,
Let's be crazy in love and surrounded by virginity,
Let's be together for now and eternity,
Or let's not, let's be involved with four walls and four walls alone,
Let's be held hostage to ourselves.
Let's.

Sally Humphries

THE WORLD SPINS ROUND

Dreaming at such a young age
where will they be
big eyes
in years from now
motor bikes on trailer
love and cared
stories of children
with no-one to share.
mothers to rush
shopping to get
little legs
pulled and stretched
daddy will listen
he's bound to do
daddy's tired
it was red with blue
door to face
pillow to talk
teddy bear
when friends are sought.
tear to tears
from year to years
children spoilt
with bought love and care
dreams can be made
when made aware
listen to colours
hear the sounds
mind yourself
the world spins round.

Stephen O'Toole

SPIRITUAL FAITH

God is a feeling from within
He comforts us for our sins
He does not judge or reprimand
He seeks only prayer from the hand
You can pray for guidance in your hour of need
But beware advice we do not always heed
We seek the usual self solution
For we are all only human
We live in a world run by greed
Regardless of colour, race, or creed
To quit the rat race and put our trust in you
Sadly there are many too few
But for those who come there is a lift
Companionship, love, understanding, the greatest gift.

Janette Homer

BEYOND THE VEIL

I am nothing,
One small particle of the human race
Held in wonder by what has been,
Awed by the great eternal space
And mysteries yet unseen.
Just a veil divides us transparent . . . thin
Hiding the wonders of tomorrow
And the next complex thing
Bringing us joy or sorrow
Will it be the prize for which we dream
Evolving endless, countless changes
Into the new world for which men scheme,
I know not the enormity of what it ranges
For I am nothing.

Dorothy Walker

RESTORATIVE POWER

The toil of my everyday life
in my soul is deeply in strife.
To survive I must have fresh air
I find my well known boots to wear.

The wind around my cheeks will bite,
the thoughts will through my head take flight
Walking the land of woods and lanes
until the pulse has cleared my brains.

The horizon is hanging low
and by my boot the river flow.
On my path I meet a moorhen,
I begin to feel good again.

I see the deer, I hear the birds,
clearly the sky shows me these words:
Into your lungs inhale the air,
be to yourself and nature fair.

I wonder off, I wonder on
before i know the day has gone.
I feel refreshed in mind and soul
and will again take up my goal.

Lisbeth Cameron

COUNTRY WALKS

Walking in the countryside,
That's where I love to be,
No matter what the season,
There is so much to see.

The winter frost turns spiders webs,
Into lace so fine
I gaze at them in wonder,
Each one a new design.

I see the buds come out in spring,
And watch the lambs at play,
Sometimes I get up early,
Before the break of day.
To see the morning sunrise,
It is a wondrous sight,
As slowly all the darkness goes,
The sky, colourful and bright.

In summer when the sky is blue,
And the sun high in the sky,
I listen to the birds that sing,
In the woods, near by.
I watch the rabbits as they run,
Sometimes I see a deer,
There are so many sights to see,
And many sounds to hear.

Beneath my feet in autumn,
A carpet made of leaves
The wind, now blowing very hard,
Is bending all the trees.

Each season there's so much to see,
In the countryside, which pleases me.

Doreen Higgs

RESCUE DOG

You came to the *Rescue*
Where people who care,
Fed me and groomed me
While I was there.

Then through the wire
I saw you stop and stare.
You took me home with you,
Now I live with you there.

We go for long walks,
Happy memories we share.
No-one will harm you -
Not while I'm there.

The cat was a stray too,
We make a good pair,
When the Tom cats annoy her
Then I am there.

You'll never have burglars,
I'm sure they won't dare,
I've a deep, warning bark
To tell them I'm there.

When you feel sad and lonely,
And life's hard to bear
I'll stay close and cheer you -
For you I'll be there.

So treat me with kindness,
And keep me with care,
For you can be certain,
I'll always be there.

A Janes

A SHADOW NEVER SEEN

I am memories, I am thought,
And all that I might be,
I am love, I am hate,
A total mass of mystery.

I long for the impossible,
And strive to reach the starlit sky,
I yearn to be unique
Although I really don't know why.

I am the shattered dreams of my past,
And the growing dreams of tomorrow,
I know one day I will die,
And at times I feel sorrow.

Pain is one of my facets
And I spar with regret,
I am a shadow never seen,
By all whom I have never met.

I am tomorrow for a while,
Or the future perhaps,
I am a face in a place
Where fate draws its maps.

I am wisdom, I am hope
Enrapt by a song,
I am here on this Earth
But I feel I don't belong.

Jack Ellis

A MARCH DAY IN METHWOLD

Fields rise,
Follow the speedway clouds
Careering around their dirt track.
Sky's engine roars,
Fires on all cylinders.

Wheelspun soil spreads wild,
Hangs on hedgerows,
Riddles the road red,
Seeding unlikely places
In deepening darkness.

Before the eyes of this Welsh mountain man
(Himself a fine bender before the wind).
From this monster month of March machine,
A full throttle Fen blow.

P Holt

BUTTERFLY

Butterflies flying
Colours ablaze
Golden rays shining
Sweet sunshine days
Flowers in springtime
Each petals a smile
Time enough to wander
Time to stop a while
When minutes last for hours
And no-one knows you're there
When happiness descends on you
From within the dewy air
Leaves that float from hedgerows
Starlings in the sky
Scents that take your breath away
If only I could fly
Free-er than the southern wind
Is how I want to be
To live and love and glide through life
A butterfly that's me.

Alison White

I HAD TO SET HIM FREE

A memory of long ago
when I was only ten
A baby hare I cared for
as he'd lost his mother then.

I nursed and fed the tiny hare
and soon he grew quite strong
So tame he was and gentle
but I did not have him long.

The time has come to let him go
is what my father said
As up the back lane very slow
my hare to freedom led.

I set him down and walked away
my heart was very sad
When I looked back, he'd followed me
I remember feeling glad.

Try again my father said
you can't keep him you know
This time when I put him down
I told him he must go.

For you are wild and must be free
to live your life alone
I put him down in long green grass
and turned to go back home.

I waited while he ran away
across the fields he sped
I knew that he was happy
for he never turned his head.

Catherine Barrons

THE NATURE GAME

When you're tired of television and your games have lost their spell
And you grumble that you don't know what to do -
That's the time to stop and listen to what Nature has to tell
Of the best pastime of all, awaiting you.
In the silence of the countryside or bustle of the town
There's a world of fascination to explore;
Just be quiet awhile and listen; stand still, and look around
At the tiny things you've never seen before.

There's a strange new world to wonder at in every seaside pool,
And a tiny jungle in a patch of grass
Where little insects crawl and creep among the shadows cool;
Have you heard the whirr of wings as starlings pass?
Or the song of birds at dawning, when the world is shining new
And each leaf and flower opens to the sun.
Have you felt the hush of evening, seen track marks in the dew,
Or watched the stars come out when day is done?

The velvet on a bumble bee, a hawk-moth's humming flight -
So many lovely things for you to see.
Have you heard grasshopper violins, or seen a glow-worm's light
Shine green and clear beneath a wayside tree?
Have you watched a spider spin a web? A miracle of skill.
Could you paint the patterns on a butterfly
With a million tiny feather flakes of coloured dust, until
It seems a living flower flutters by?

Don't touch or chase or frighten them: remember, there's a rule -
You vow to care for every living thing.
You couldn't make an acorn in the woodwork class at school,
Or tune a blackbird's music in the spring.
The Nature Game has prizes too, You'll learn to feel a part
Of a glorious changing pattern without end -
And as you travel onward with affection in your heart
Each furred and feathered creature is your friend.

Audrey Forbes-Handley

BRASS BAND IN MUKER

Muker, where road and river meet
Near Kisdon Force, and gorge and hill descend
By cottage steps and gardens,
Sweet with summer scents,
Down to the village square.

There, one August Sunday afternoon
We came, descending from high hills above the Swale,
From where we watched the river winding down
To Ivelet and the old corpse way;
And on to Richmond Castle holding sway
Above the town with cobbled wynds
And misty moors so far away.

We came then to this lovely place
Where windows face the south to catch the sun,
As lazily it plays with shadows from the leafy trees.
Expecting there to find the day asleep
And all the world at home.

But turning by the Chapel Hall,
We came upon the unexpected sound
Of Verdi from a small brass band,
Which, attracting all
In quiet content, created a retreat
For refugees like us from cities pall.

A sleepy village; some would say in slow decay,
From days when Swaledale's mines
Caused men to burrow in the hills for lead.
Now they are dead, whose spirits still survive
In Verdi's music from a village band.

Ron Woollard